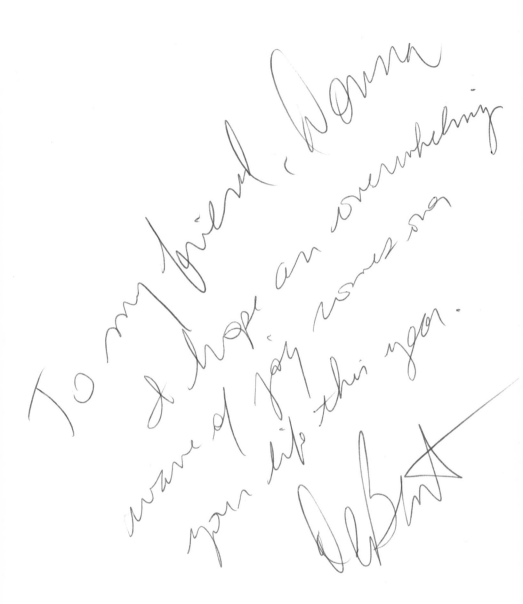

To my friend, Donna
I hope an overwhelming
wave of joy rushes into
your life this year.

# THE
# VIRTUAL
# EXECUTIVE

## How to Act Like a CEO
## Online and Offline

### D. A. BENTON

NEW YORK   CHICAGO   SAN FRANCISCO
LISBON   LONDON   MADRID   MEXICO CITY   MILAN
NEW DELHI   SAN JUAN   SEOUL   SINGAPORE
SYDNEY   TORONTO

**The McGraw·Hill Companies**

Copyright ©2012 by Debra A. Benton. All rights reserved. Printed in the United States of America. Except as permitted under the United States Copyright Act of 1976, no part of this publication may be reproduced or distributed in any form or by any means, or stored in a data base or retrieval system, without the prior written permission of the publisher.

1 2 3 4 5 6 7 8 9 0 QFR/QFR 1 8 7 6 5 4 3 2

ISBN: 978-0-07-178715-4
MHID: 0-07-178715-1

e-ISBN: 978-0-07-178716-1
e-MHID: 0-07-178716-X

McGraw-Hill books are available at special quantity discounts to use as premiums and sales promotions, or for use in corporate training programs. To contact a representative, please e-mail us at bulksales@mcgraw-hill.com.

This book is printed on acid-free paper.

# CONTENTS

# PREFACE

In 1991, I fell in love with, and later married, a cowboy. No, not a Dallas Cowboy or a pejorative "Wall Street cowboy" or a rhinestone one either, but a real mountain living, cattle wrangling, horse riding, rattlesnake killing, country music lovin', cowboy-hat-and-boot-wearing cowboy.

He personifies the best of the stereotypical ol' West cowboys, the ones you see in the classic John Wayne or Gary Cooper movies whose work requires perspiration, not regulation. He isn't interested so much in rules but rather principles, values, and character. He listens and observes more than he talks. He speaks up when others are afraid to; takes action when others don't. His word means he'll do what he says.

If things get tough—physically or mentally—he doesn't quit on you. His unbendable code keeps his promises and doesn't dodge and spin it or gripe. With a happy head, heart, and face, he speaks straightforward and decisively. He doesn't much go for windbags or people who are mean or petty. He radiates decency. He makes tough decisions without looking over his shoulder or worrying what someone else will think. He gets his strength from knowing what is right and what is wrong and being true to his beliefs. One of his favorite sayings is, "A man with courage makes a majority."

His personality offered me the *life* partner that I wanted. The problem became executing the *work* that I do and love.

It turns out cowboys do not need a lot of indoor space. To be with him meant I took residence on a remote high mountain ranch in a 550-square-foot, 75-year-old cabin heated only by a wood-burning stove. It came complete with outhouse, sporadic electricity, no running water in the winter, no cell phone service, and no landline phone service either, though we did get a landline installed shortly after I moved in.

Prior to meeting the cowboy, I was weighing office space in New York and San Francisco to accommodate my executive coaching and training company. Then cupid popped into the picture, and I settled into a ranch with boundaries measured in miles not acres, where it was seven miles to the adjacent neighbor.

There was no office water cooler, company cafeteria, or Starbucks on the corner to dart into for a latte with a prospective client. Nearly 200 miles to the closest metropolitan airport and 60 miles from an urban area meant that I didn't drive in for the Chamber of Commerce after-hours networking event, nor did I drop in on my accountant to ask some questions, nor did I even grocery shop except once a week when we made a trek into town. Yet I had to run my company—a consulting business with accounts in 19 different countries and client companies in all major U.S. cities. My computer worked slowly—landline, remember. Moreover, that was only when the electricity was on. If there was a problem down the line, we were at the end in getting it resolved.

In 1994, I chose to be removed from daily or frequent face-to-face interpersonal communication for lifestyle and love. I had to learn to work successfully in a whole new way. That meant I still had to manage my team and interact with my clients but with little face time.

I ended up being virtual before virtual was cool.

In my first year living on the ranch and working away from in-person contact, I relied on the effective leadership skills I teach and the technology available to me then. As a result, my corporation brought in more money than it had in its 15-year-history. Fortunately, this trend continues to this day.

Twenty-plus years later, 76 percent of the workforce works in a virtual fashion of some sort—this book is for you.

# ACKNOWLEDGMENTS

I t's almost unfair that my name is on this book because the inspiration, motivation, and information came from others.

First, Rodney Sweeney (the cowboy) gets a special thanks, of course. My parents, Fred and Teresa Benton, taught me about being a solid citizen: good-natured, undaunted, hardworking.

Zachery Gajewski, my editor at McGraw-Hill, provided exceptional advice and direction that kept me on track. And Fortier Public Relations got the word out.

Scott Regan of Apigee and Allison Saltzer of Microsoft came up with the premise for this book.

And the many people who answered my questions and shared their experiences are listed in alphabetical order. If ranked in importance, they'd all be number one:

| | | |
|---|---|---|
| Ana Arias | Ivan Campuzano | Christopher Felder |
| Lynn Batara | Alan Carlson | Dan Fennell |
| Sally Beatty | Karen Castranova | Laura Fernandez |
| Norbert Beatty | Ann Clark | Bradley Fortin |
| Devon Beitzel | Lisa Conboy | Mark Fortier |
| Bob Berkowitz | Todd DeWitt | Wil Gettys |
| Greg Brail | Jack Falvey | Craig Green |

| | | |
|---|---|---|
| Joel Goetl | Suzie Mills | Tracy Stevens |
| Rene Gomez | Scott Metzger | Rudy Tauscher |
| Robin Herron | Amy Motto | Nathan Teegarten |
| Chelsea Harrison | Alfred Matter | Christopher Tucker |
| Katarina Hicks | Adil Nemat | Sarah J. Turner |
| Sandy Hogan | Daina Penikas | Inge Trump |
| Steven Israel | Leila Porteous | Donna Uchida |
| Sue Johnk | Sherry Pudlaski | Matthew Villalobos |
| Ki Johnson | Mary Reed | Emma Williams |
| Chet Kapoor | Steve Schell | Killian Williams |
| Tarah Keech | Elizabeth Schorre | Brooke Weinstein |
| Regina Kenney | Sandra Shoemaker | Ben Westdorp |
| John Krebbs | John Slagle | Joann Woy |
| Lawrence Land | Daniel Smith | |
| Susan Masters | Gary Stern | |

And a big thanks to my Yoda, Curtis Rex Carter.

# INTRODUCTION

*My goal is to give you simplicity in a world of complexity.*
—D. A. Benton

It's estimated that by 2015 the workforce will be composed of approximately one-third millennials, one-third generation Xers, and one-third baby boomers—with a few traditionalists not ready to walk off the playing field. It could get funky. The only digital interpersonal relationship and communication rule will be: there are no clear rules.

You will be in one of those generational groups. Regardless of your age or time in the workplace, in your pursuit to be better, you will still have to separate yourself from contenders in a competitive environment. That goes whether you are working face-to-face or on your laptop, desktop, tablet, or mobile device. You have to put yourself out there, elevate your game, and stand out even when others can't see you physically.

So, how do you differentiate yourself from others in a cyberworld? How do you craft a masterful message to establish a unique executive brand? How do you take that up a notch? What are the little things that make people think of you? How do you make them remember you for the right reasons? How do you put your best foot forward in the virtual business space? And how important is it really to take the physical experience and replace it with a virtual one?

The truth is, you cannot ignore the virtual world.

Well, maybe you can, until some embarrassing or inappropriate footage of you gets posted online and your next job title ends up being "assistant to the summer intern" while you get written off with three words: "considered not ready."

*"If you want to avoid becoming obsolete in the twenty-first century, you had better get really skilled with today's technology or sleep with someone who is."*

**A NOTE TO MY READERS**

The set-apart quotes sprinkled throughout the book are from CEOs, CTOs, CMOs, CIOs, CFOs, CPOs, entrepreneurs, free agents, techie geeks, MBA students, some business misfits, and a professional dropout or two that I interviewed for this book. They are virtual executives from the United States as well as New Zealand, Afghanistan, South Korea, the Czech Republic, China, Japan, India, Scotland, and Belgium. They expressed themselves so clearly that I didn't want to muddy their comments with any rewriting.

No matter your age or the stage of your career, you have to be unsurpassed at your job: brilliant, inspiring, authentic, skilled, undaunted, composed, honest, and a good example to emulate. And to be a contender today, you must be that same person uniformly online as well as offline. If you don't embrace all modes of communication at your disposal, you will fall behind so badly you may never catch up. With electronic and digital communication, we might all look the same—except where we make an effort to differentiate ourselves. We are inventing new forms of communication and technologies all the time so I am not attempting to detail the latest advances available to you—those are better covered in a blog, web page post, or online article—but rather helping you fine-tune your attitude and approach in utilizing technology.

*"Today, you have the WWW: where there is a will, there is a way."*

(Note: In every chapter, the Online/Offline sections like this one provide professional development essentials required for you to move up and ahead in your career and to go back and forth without a glitch between working face-to-face or monitor to monitor. Consider this material timeless because it consists of behind-the-scenes attitudes, values, and actions that will help you succeed as a CEO or in another leadership position, online and offline in the new digital age.)

**ONLINE/OFFLINE: WHAT IT TAKES TO BE SUCCESSFUL**

There are only two reasons to read self-help books: to become more successful and to make more money. If those are your goals, I hope this tome helps.

To benefit fully from *The Virtual Executive*, it helps to understand what successful means. My definition of it stems from a professional career spanning over 35 enjoyable years working with CEOs and their organizations. From a myriad of experiences, I've found some things to be universally true about individual success.

For example, the ultimate personal triumph can be one of these moments:

- You are working toward, you are on the brink of, or you have achieved your dream career goals *while* you remain a solid citizen. You are viewed as a "good" person: responsible, honest, and fair. You have not, will not, and do not let the business political system corrupt you. The upshot is that your coworkers truly like, trust, and respect you, and your family members do too.

- When you communicate—which you have to do all of the time with everyone in some manner or another—you are deemed impressive, memorable, credible, genuine, trusted, liked, competent, confident, comfortable, cool, calm, and collected. You set a good example of personal leadership, and you help infuse it in others.

- You feel broadly adequate, and you treat others as broadly adequate too. That means you expect acceptance for what you bring to the table (which doesn't mean you are owed anything) and you give it to others. You choose to accept the motives and character of others; you do not judge. Any and every one gets the benefit of the doubt until the person absolutely, unequivocally, indisputably, and undeniably proves to merit otherwise in motive and character. Even then, you do not stand in judgment; you just separate yourself from him or her. That means you fire the person if it is a subordinate; quit or get out from under if it's your boss; or separate yourself if it's a friend or colleague.

- People do not care if your style is dictatorial or participative so much; they care because you have goodwill toward them.

- You fully appreciate the Golden Online/Offline Rule "Do unto others as you'd have them do unto you." You limit inappropriate, incorrect, flat-out bad behavior, and you don't attack a person's character or motive.

- You understand that when others treat you negatively, it's because they themselves feel inadequate, do not feel "okay," are having a bad day, or are upset, and they often attempt to transfer those feelings onto others. However, you do not let them do that to you.

- You are equally effective in communicating these positive

attributes that have contributed to your success whether you are face-to-face, talking on a phone, or e-mailing halfway around the world.

The foundation in mindset just described is what it takes to be successful. It's what separates you from others in the same quest.

## YOUR (AND MY) WORLD IS ONE OF COMPLETE RESPONSIBILITY BUT INCOMPLETE CONTROL

So what do you need to do to succeed in this day and age? You need to be able to move seamlessly between the multitudes of demands from many directions:

- The C-suite executive who wants to meet face-to-face
- The senior manager who requires a videoconference call with you and project members in São Paulo, Tokyo, and Toledo
- The junior manager who writes you a flurry of e-mails
- The new-hire who sends you a blizzard of text messages

Traditionally, business has been done in person and face-to-face, where others can see your great jaw line and experience your firm handshake. However, being in the flesh is fairly restrictive compared to the various communication channels available to you today.

With video on their smart phones, tablets, or laptops, people you conduct business with can still see your eyes and your nervous or relaxed body language; observe your shining or frowning facial expression; experience your charisma; and hear your melodious or monotone voice. While talking, listening, watching, and interacting with you, they also can do an Internet search and instantly find photos or video of you, read reports whose development you've taken part in, or read about projects you've been involved in, hear your voice in speeches, and scan articles you've written or in which you've been quoted. They can access online communities to read your professional profile, likes, people you follow, and those who follow you. Today, you can blog, post or comment on a website, tag, e-mail, text message, or videochat at any time to not only find out about others but also to show more of who you are.

*"When I Google individuals or view their social networking posting history, I get to see if they are one-shot-hotshot-empty-suits or sustained solid citizens. As my dad used to say, 'The years carve an individual in different ways.'"*

You have the option to utilize all kinds of communication, both online and offline. Online trumps offline all to heck though because the Internet's great number of communication channels increases your chance of actually communicating with others. In contrast to offline communication modes, the Internet offers a greater possibility of hearing others and being heard.

Facts
▶ 6 out of 7 American homes have broadband Internet service.
▶ 9 out of 10 Americans are online.
(Note: Sources for "Fact Sidebars" found on page 239)

You don't need to be in the flesh to demonstrate your brilliance, skill, and character; you just need electricity to power up and recharge your devices.

### THE BENEFITS OF ONLINE COMMUNICATION

You get things done a whole lot faster, cheaper, and with less effort across time zones and geographic distances and to a larger number of people. If a person that you need to interact with can't or won't right now, you can send an e-mail or text message or leave a voice mail. And ditto from him or her to you.

You have a world of information a click away. It used to be that politicians, global leaders, and CEOs of multinationals owned the bulk of information access. With the Internet, you can gain just as much data, just as fast as anyone. You have accessibility to the same knowledge as anyone else in the world.

**There is a less instant prejudice and bias** based on physical things that (unfairly) but stereotypically might work against you like short/tall, handsome/homely, slow/fast, skinny/heavyset, or young/old.

*"My hair is thinning at a rate that annoys me, and I'm going soft around the middle, but no one sees. I like that. I can hide my tears and sweaty handshake plus work naked at home. Furthermore, I don't have to smell the person in the office cubicle next to me who pumps 29 sprays of cologne on himself before he goes to lunch—and, yes, I counted."*

**You don't have to respond in real time** as you would if you were facing someone in person. You can take a moment or two to mull over your reactions, collect your thoughts, read the notes that others can't see you have laid out in front of you, and be organized to position yourself however you want in a phone call, e-mail, or voice or text message.

**You can truly absorb what the other person is saying** when you don't have to engage in the physicality of face-to-face, such as mirroring, matching, pacing, or posturing. You can focus on what is being said on the phone or written on the monitor. Government-trained professional problem solvers separate themselves in rooms when trying to come up with solutions. In-person human dynamics impede creativity when people take the power chair and try to intimidate others by using overbearing body movements, measurably raising or lowering their voice, pounding the table, and so on. Digital discussions are more democratic.

**You can be communicating anytime and anywhere** in the world without having to pack a bag, drive to the airport, make it through a TSA pat down, sit squashed for three hours in an airplane seat between two passengers who should have been cut off three beers ago, and taxi to the meeting, only to find it postponed or canceled. Electronic gadgets eliminate downtime.

**Online you have software that enables you to translate languages** so you don't have semantics issues the way you do in person.

**You have many more options to present yourself,** your expertise, positions, and opinions through your web page posts, profiles, blogs, tweets, and videos. Those same sources allow you to be vetted easily. Since people learn and are influenced in various ways, you can give them a mixture of approaches—seeing, reading, listening, experiencing, and getting others' opinions.

**There are more opportunities to be monitored online than there are in person.** When observed, recorded, and documented, you get more opportunities for feedback. When you work with that feedback, you improve.

**You get a little mystique around you.** Leaving some elements unknown about each other levels the playing field. It also can break down hierarchies, encourage a little audacity, and provide some positive anticipation.

**Anonymity gives you bravery.** You can express your true opinions without having to face others. This, of course, is a double-edged sword because you might say or do something you wouldn't normally since you don't have to eyeball the person or group to whom you're speaking!

**You save trees.** And when you use less paper, you require less filing. You also experience less paper degradation from age, bugs, or dogs' eating it.

**Your community benefits from having a workforce that works**

**virtually** when you take into account the amount of reduced automobile emissions and traffic on roads, increased public safety, decreased number of parking lots, and increased space for vegetation.

**Your company benefits through** increased job satisfaction and productivity and decreased workplace real estate costs, energy use, and other fixed expenses.

## TO BE A GOOD EXECUTIVE, YOU HAVE TO BE ADEPT IN ALL COMMUNICATION CHANNELS

Technical savvy alone will not make you a good executive. You will also need to be a good person and a hard worker with common sense and good people skills. If you do not have such qualities, no amount of practical, technological understanding will save you. If you do possess all these traits, you have to demonstrate them not only in your face-to-face interactions but also in your text messages, e-mails, phone conversations, video chats, and digital networking.

*"Times have changed due to technology but human nature remains the same."*

In two of my previous books, *Executive Charisma: Six Steps to Mastering the Art of Leadership* (McGraw-Hill), and *CEO Material: How to Be a Leader in Any Organization* (McGraw-Hill), I fully discuss conventional, in-person communication. In this book, I explore the online presentation of self and how to manage and lead using the communication channels open to you. I am not writing as a technologist; if I tried that, my book would be outdated before you finish your dinner this evening. I'm writing as your coach to give you better ways to use electronic gadgets to get the things done that you need to as you seamlessly move between online and offline communication.

**ONLINE/OFFLINE: BE A SOLID CITIZEN**

Having upright character is entirely self-serving: You feel good about yourself, and you sleep soundly. You don't fear how your actions will look in the newspaper or in the blogosphere. You need not agonize over how your kids, partner, parents, friends, classmates, neighbors, and coworkers will view you. Being a solid citizen is the ultimate destressor. Consider these three truths:

- Fame, popularity, and riches go away; only character endures.
- Ethos is established at the top, and you're the top in your world.
- People want to trust you, so make it easy for them to, especially when they can't see you.

*"I have plenty of faults, but I try to do the right thing."*

Your upbringing, socialization, religious training, and cultural environment affect your predisposition. But you choose whom you want to be going forward; it's your decision at this point in time. Upright actions are all due to you. You have possession of your life when you own up to personal responsibility. You don't when you won't. Your decisions as they relate to character become your moral fiber.

*"There are two reasons to do the right thing: (1) A sense of right and wrong. (2) You're going to get caught if you don't."*

Eight days a week you will encounter temptation to break your personal code of conduct. One college conducted a sting to test for cheating. Of the 600 students who took the test, one-third cheated. When a student was interviewed about his cheating, he said, "What's the big deal? Everybody does it all the time."

*"The true test of character is doing the right thing even when no one sees."*

To do what's right, you merely make one of two choices: be honest or be dishonest. That's it. It's not complicated.

And you don't:

- Intentionally mislead
- Straddle the line
- Disseminate false information
- Break promises
- Go back on your word
- Waltz around
- Exaggerate
- Participate in other chicanery

Also, these words do not come out of your mouth or get put into an e-mail:

Everyone else does it.

It's a victimless crime.

I can hide it.

It doesn't matter how it gets done. I just have to get it done.

Well, maybe just this one time . . .

No one will ever know.

I'll just shred (or burn) that document.

What's in it for me?

How much can we get away with?

I'd say anything goes.

I will deny we had this discussion.

We didn't have this conversation.

This is a nonmeeting.

Is this legal?

*"Nothing baffles people full of tricks and duplicities more than simple straightforward integrity."*

So if you signed Oprah's No Phone Zone Pledge, the national campaign started in 2009 against texting or talking on your cell phone while driving, you shouldn't do any of these things behind the wheel either: scratch off a lottery ticket, read the Bible, eat a bowl of cereal, change your clothes, or paint your fingernails despite the fact those activities (all of which I've seen people do) are not stated in the pledge.

The far end of lacking integrity is breaking the law. There are corporate scoundrels who are involved in insider stock trading, securities fraud, wire fraud, money laundering, bribes, Ponzi schemes, and kickbacks (just a short list of potential options). People steal, cheat, and lie online and off. Experts report that today cybercrime is more prevalent than drug crime.

In this day and age, you will be found out. You might go to jail. You will lose trust from family and friends, and you will never get it back—even when you are being truthful.

Integrity is pretty simple: show up, get in fast with the truth, let go of the outcome.

*"Sometimes liars end up as bosses, but they are likely to last only a year, not a career."*

Facts
♦ We are lied to up to 200 times a day.
♦ Maybe that's why the United States has 5 percent of the world population but 66 percent of the world's lawyers.

## FOUR ACTIONS OF A DYNAMIC VIRTUAL PRESENCE

There are basically two kinds of information:

1. Data
2. Anything pertaining to self

The first type is self-explanatory. The second type of information is what you hear first, remember longest, and act on the most and fastest. Just as information that pertains to others is what they hear first, remember longest, and act on the most and fastest. So find out what that information is. Effective online communication delivers empathy; it says that you understand and you care. Within the first 20 seconds of a face-to-face meeting and first 2 seconds of a phone call or e-mail, you have to give the person the number two type of information.

*"In detached communication, you need to get better at how to get better."*

To effectively connect and present yourself online, *ask* early and often of those with whom you deal: "How do *you* prefer to communicate?" Then use the channel that person prefers even if it is not the one you prefer.

One CEO I interviewed for this book had an aversion to cell phones and e-mail and preferred leaving voice messages using his iPad. Another CEO preferred yellow stickie notes left on his desk for incoming messages. And a different one installed—in 2011—a loudspeaker system in his company headquarters over which he broadcasted everything from simple directives to the latest news several times a day.

So one good potential **first action** to having a dynamic presence in a virtual workplace is to find out the preferred communication channel of the person, or people, you are speaking with and then accommodating that preference.

A **second action** is to strive for the common theme, the "something" that connects you together no matter how far apart—age, experience, culture, language, geography, and the rest that could be separators instead of unite-*ers*.

A **third action** is for you to consistently and persistently work to leave a positive lasting impression regardless of the communication channel you use. Although technology enables you to do things more quickly, to bond and connect today, you will get further faster by being slower and more deliberate in your communication. There is a time and a place for making phone calls or sending text messages or e-mails, having video chats, or using social networks. Pick the right one based on what type of information, type 1 or type 2, you are conveying.

With our sophisticated technological advances, it is easy to lose sight of the human aspect of communication because we do not have to face people and actually see them in the flesh. People attempt to process you and treat you like a commodity or transaction as compared to developing meaningful interactions. It's up to you not only to fight the urge to do that yourself but also to resist allowing others to do it to you. That's your **fourth action.**

The following chapters will help you communicate effectively using others' preferred channels as well as your own. They will help you seek affinity with other people and make sincere connections. They will help you be the best that's in you and then make that better. And they will help you make your missives personal and focused on people, not processes.

As you read this book, feel free to e-mail me with your own insights and experiences (debra@debrabenton.com). Keep in mind throughout that technology means little compared to *you* as a human being. Everything you do needs to generate trust because that is what people are looking for from you online and off.

# CHAPTER 1

# Voice Channels

Mobile devices and smart phones are obviously not just for talking. You can use them to check e-mail; listen to music; play games; watch videos; download and display TV shows; browse the web; schedule and organize your calendar; get voice-guided directions; and take and send photos and videos. The cell phone is a watch, an alarm clock, a stopwatch, a calculator, an address book, a wallet to pay for bar-coded purchases, and a portal to access thousands of apps. It's pretty much up to the human imagination as to what one can do with a mobile device today, let alone in the future!

> *"A self-defense expert taught me that if people are acting suspiciously around me, I should hold up my phone toward them and say they're live on the phone and being recorded. That generally stops them."*

The drawback of mobile devices is that you are undeniably reachable at all times, and you have an obligation to respond. There is a perceived accessibility expected seven days out of seven. Senders hold an implied connectedness whether you want to be reached or not.

*"The only relief I get from the cell phone is when I'm in the dentist chair. I've found myself looking forward to those appointments."*

A cell phone, however, is for *your* convenience. You don't have to be a slave to it or be at its disposal. One time I overheard some people weighing which bike trail to take and ask, "Which has the best cell phone reception?" I think that's just not right. Such technology should improve our lives, not become a distraction.

Facts
♦ 27 percent of U.S. homes do not have a landline.
♦ 23 percent are likely to give up the landline in the near future.

### USING YOUR MOBILE DEVICE

Unless your phone is bugged, it's generally a good communication channel for discussing confidential information, touchy subjects, and sensitive issues. If you have bad news or things are getting tense and you need to challenge, correct, or disapprove of someone's behavior, the phone is better than putting it in writing. If there is anything that could be misinterpreted in writing, or if you need to reduce the risk of being misread, use the phone. Also, though it shows more nerve to deliver bad news in person, it is not always possible, so the phone is the next best option.

With an oral exchange, you have a better chance of getting people to tell you what's on their mind than when communication is being screened through a written channel. Furthermore, intonation helps you convey appreciation for the time and attention of the people you are talking with.

Fact
♦ 18 percent of people fake a phone call to avoid having to interact with others.

**ONLINE/OFFLINE: PREPARE BEFORE YOU MEET, TALK, OR CLICK**
You can be anything and do anything with enough preparation and work. To be effective in what message you want to get across to

others, you must prepare. If you painstakingly prepare more than most people bother to, it will measurably improve your chances of affecting people the way you want. Some CEOs tell me that for every hour they expect to be in front of someone, they give themselves two to three hours of preparation.

Preparation increases confidence and optimism and makes you more interesting to whomever you are speaking with. People respond well to someone who is sure of what he or she wants and goes for it. Before you communicate, ask yourself, "What do I want to accomplish in this exchange? What are the reasons to do this—both implicit and explicit? Why should he or she give a darn? What is the likely outcome of this exchange?" And then, after it's done ask, "Did I accomplish what I set out to?"

Fact
♦ The rule of thumb of courtiers in Buckingham Palace is that "a one-minute visit with the queen requires three hours of planning."

### SOME TIPS ON BEING PREPARED

Seek info in advance, not at the last minute. Download history surrounding the topic. Consider the current environment. Study the tendencies of people involved. Focus on the people at the other end of the line—your audience of one or a hundred. Think about what they want to know and why it's important to them.

Overly prepare. Do your homework to the $n$th degree. Think about, mull over, ruminate, and weigh anything you should consider about the facts, the project, the different angles, and the perspectives of people involved. Write down and analyze options.

**Understand the other people's fears, dreams, and desires**. Figure out the big drivers. It's all about them: where they are coming from, their fears, and their nightmares. See life from their point of view (POV) so they think "this person gets me."

**Facts and figures are important, but feelings count.** More decisions are made for emotional reasons than factual.

**Role-play in your mind or even on paper.** What will the other parties ask? What will they say? What will they bring up that is important to them?

**Answer, to yourself, every question you might get asked before it is posed.** Supervisors or executives will grill you with questions so you might as well ask yourself ahead of time and think through the answer. When the real question comes, it may not be friendly or nice, but your prethinking will have reduced your stress.

**Every time you communicate, practice being smooth.** You might think you can stumble all around with a friend and it doesn't make a difference. Wrong. Everything you do is training your brain, so even with friends, try for improved conversing.

**Do not dismiss serious preparation as overkill for a simple phone call and just assume you can wing it.** Take a deep breath before you start talking. It helps when your lungs are full of air. And as one CEO told me, "Put on your power shoes and really pay attention."

**Stop pondering after you've absorbed what you can.** Decide on the point where no additional information, no cramming, no more thinking is going to help.

*"So few people make the extra effort; if you do, that's really the reason you'll get noticed."*

In an age of instant responses, you may need to remind yourself to slow down and think things through. It's nice to be fast, but instant responses can prove to be disastrous. Consider others' questions and interests; then plan a response. Yes, I know you have limited time and limited resources to do this, but if you don't slow down, pause, and prepare, you will be unable to present yourself, statements, or points clearly. If you seem unprepared, you show a lack of care toward the other party or the outcome of the discussion. Make sure to:

- Slow down.
- Get in the moment.

- Consider your audience.
- Construct a message.

The higher you go in your career, the more preparation is required, so you might as well get in the habit early. And it's never too early to start: I have heard of a job website that helps eighth-graders prepare for their career.

## ONE-ON-ONE PHONE CALLS

With so many ways to reach people, a direct phone call out of the blue can be considered rude and disruptive by some. Many have told me that they prefer a text message inquiring, "Are you able to talk now?" or an appointment call time arranged via e-mail.

### *KNOW YOUR PHONE'S FEATURES*

Know how to use the features on your phone before you make and take calls, especially if you have a new device. It is annoying and waste of time for people on the other end of the line when you accidentally cut them off or tell them to wait as you learn to transfer the call or put on the speaker.

It's also pretty embarrassing if you think you put a call on hold but didn't and the person can hear your conversation. This situation has the potential to become your personal Wikileaks moment. For example, a financial advisor I know was talking to his client by phone. The advisor thought he had hung up when he pushed the wrong feature to answer an incoming call. He ended up in an accidental three-way call, with the clients overhearing pejorative comments between the two advisors about the client. Needless to say, that professional affiliation was soon severed.

Practice how to properly use the device in advance, not while someone is on the other end of the line. People will tolerate poor quality sound and functionality when unavoidable, but they will think you're lazy if you don't control what you can. There is also a risk that a lot of what you think you communicated will have been lost.

Facts
♦ 67 percent of all calls are considered less important than the work they interrupt.
♦ 50 percent of all calls are longer than they need to be to exchange information due to chitchat about weather, vacations, and weekends.

### CONSIDER YOUR SURROUNDINGS
Be aware of background noise when you're going to make or take a phone call. If you want to be fully understood, use a landline for better transmission so as to minimize static and dropped calls. I had more clarity in a landline phone call from Kabul, Afghanistan, than I had from a cell phone call from Silicon Valley last week.

Be aware when multitasking and clicking away on your keyboard that you can easily be heard; it's disrespectful, no matter how talented or capable you are in doing it. One human resources manager told me she lost interest in a job candidate that she was interviewing when she kept hearing him type away; he even took another call at one point. In defense of the candidate, if he was taking notes about the interview, he should have said, "Do you mind if I'm typing some information you're giving me? That's how I take notes. I'm fully engaged with you in this conversation, but you might hear the keystrokes, and I don't want you to think otherwise."

Another good rule to remember about your surroundings: don't talk on the phone in the bathroom; it's gross.

**ONLINE/OFFLINE: GRIN AND BEAR IT**
Smile when you pick up or click on the phone, and continue to smile as you talk regardless of who's calling or what the conversation is about. The person on the other end of the line can hear a smile, and she can also hear a frown, smirk, and rolling of the eyes. Your articulation improves when your jaw is loosened up; your voice

intonation and cadence are more appealing; and you're less likely to be boringly dull.

Your telephone voice is the equivalent of the in-person body language people use to size you up. They hear your sincerity, passion, enthusiasm, conviction—your personality—or lack thereof, in your voice. Their positive reading of you gets you set for a more positive outcome; similarly, a negative reading can start you off on the wrong foot, annoy the other person, hurt your personal reputation and the reputation of your company, and cost you a connection.

Have a calm intensity tone and tempo when speaking in person, on the phone, or on video. Your voice should be audible, modulated, and matter-of-fact sounding. It should be steady and even-keeled, without useless filler words (ah, uh, umh, okay, and so on). I call it a *pass-the-salt tone of voice:* no matter how excited or agitated you might be, you still usually have even tone of voice when you ask across the table for the salt. The expression is just a mnemonic device to remind you to speak the way you'd like to be spoken to. Fast, high, shrill, studiously slow, singsong, brusque, too quiet, or too loud—each sends its own emotional message, and generally not a positive one.

*"Your words should be like canned green beans—soft and tender— not like corn nuts. It makes it easier if you have to eat them later."*

When you talk on the phone to new people, you form a picture in your mind about what they look like. They are doing the identical thing about you at the same time. Since you cannot look them in the eye to show that you're paying singular attention, they have to hear over the phone line that you are listening. They can tell when you are fidgeting and not giving undivided concentration. Using one wrong word, phrase, or tone because you are speaking too fast or are not concentrating will ding their trust in you.

*"I've found that the fastest one is the weakest and most insecure."*

There will be times when you're speaking to someone and, although you are under control, the other person isn't. As the conversation gets more heated, both of your voices can end up louder and faster. Stop it for your benefit as well as the other person's. Rein yourself in and immediately slow your pace, and volume, way down. Regain the small smile. You'll calm yourself and others and have a more productive conversation.

*"I was nicknamed Darth Vader behind my back among my team members because I usually forgot to mute and I was always breathing heavily while I was hovering over the microphone."*

You don't need a wide smile, a snapshot pose, a big 'ole rubber beam, or a wolfish grin. Rather, you need just a slightly open mouth with a friendly upturn of the lips—a small smile. The demeanor I'm promoting is an undaunted, comfortable-in-your-skin, shiny business game face. Consider the following:

- A shiny face from your attitude, not from perspiration, transmits well across cultures.
- Smiling isn't about happiness (although I hope you are). It's about confidence and taking responsibility for the energy you bring to the place.
- Your small smile makes you look awake, alert, alive, implacable, and approachable.
- You can have a determined jaw but still have a small smile—your expression will only enhance the keen intelligence in your eyes.
- If you smile, you can't as easily chew gum, eat, or drink (which obviously needs to be nixed) because every saliva slap against your jaw is exaggerated in the person's ear.
- Not smiling causes inaccurate responses to you. You'll have an uphill battle without even realizing it.

*"When I walk in to a board meeting, I put on a game face and smile. Then I imagine I'm on a high dive and I leap off."*

Maintain your smiling expression while talking and listening on the phone, driving, walking down the hall, eating, texting—regardless of whether you're mad, glad, scared, tired, or stressed. Keep your small smile regardless of the other people's attitudes during conversations. If you shift your attitude because the people you are speaking with appear unreceptive, you are letting them control you. Besides, you don't know what they are thinking. Maybe they are receptive, but they haven't notified their face yet.

In person, some people will "test" your smile by returning a nonreceptive frown back at you to see if you will drop it. Don't. Keep at it. When you use a neutral small smile, you are more approachable, and people are more likely to tell you what you need to know. But if you set your jaw, frown, or look disapproving, they will back away from the conversation.

*"I caught myself not breaking a smile until 3 p.m. one day, and I decided I needed to get a different job."*

If your mouth turns down from habit, laziness, focused attention, lack of awareness, age, or weak facial muscles, you look and sound bored, uninterested, and uninteresting. One man told me, "I'm married. I don't have to smile." "Hmmm," was all I chose to say.

Keep the small smile. That's the single most important indicator of confidence. Maintain the awake, alert, alive facial expression when you're talking and listening, even when you're not physically in front of other people. Most people tend to look animated and interested when they themselves are talking, and then let their face drop into a slack or pursed lip expression when others are talking. Avoid this habit because if you don't, it will look like you believe what you have to say is more important and that those who are speaking are boring you.

*MAKE THE CALL*

When you are the originator of the call, know what you want as the outcome. If you don't know where you're going in the conversation, how will you know you got there? Be prepared to talk without fumbling around when the other party picks up. If she doesn't answer, you'll be ready to leave a nonrambling message.

To increase the chance of her taking your call and having the time to talk, be interesting and worth talking to so she will pick up. Prepare to have something to say that adds value, and say it with an attitude of good cheer. When she answers, take a slight pause to slow yourself down, and then, with a small smile on your face, give a verbal handshake. "Good morning, Carol. This is Rashid calling. Did I get you at a good time?" Or ask, "Do you have a few minutes to talk?"

> *"People need to improve their phone etiquette. They call and say, 'I'd like to talk to Glenn (my boss),' and my reaction is, 'I bet you would!' They should say, 'Good morning. How are you? I'm so and so, and I'd like to talk to Glenn if he is available.' They would have a lot better chance of getting put through."*

By the way, if someone calls you and asks the "Do you have a minute?" question, an appreciated response is, "I'll take one."

If she says that she has time to talk, continue the verbal handshake with anything pertaining to her. Good humor works, as do questions. The conversation point of interest could be a comment that you remember from the last exchange you had with the person (it's flattering that you recollect) or something you learned from a social media post or Internet search on the person.

Let her respond, then transition into what you are phoning about and what you would like to get out of the conversation.

Your words and tone must have a presence and appeal, and they must stand apart from others so people are compelled to stop, listen, and want more. Simply show you care about someone or something other than yourself.

The presence, appeal, and standing apart come from an attitude and choice of pre–thought about words that communicate, "I understand your needs, and I want to work with you or help you help yourself."

Just as you shake hands in person when you enter, you shake hands when you leave, right? So give similarly at the end of the phone conversation. "Thank you for your time. I have a clearer view of what we need to do next. I'll keep you posted." Then refer back to the personal exchange from the beginning. By personalizing the call with something of interest to her, you take the edge off the intrusion into her day.

**ONLINE/OFFLINE: USING HUMOR IN PERSONAL INTERACTION**

If you don't have a sense of humor, get one. You will not succeed without it. Many CEOs have told me they see humor as a test as to whether they want to work with and be around certain people. Good leaders aggressively seek out an amusing angle in dealing with others, whether through light humor in a serious situation or the careful use of irony.

*"A person with humor mainly takes the doubt level down a notch and the trust level up."*

Bringing appropriate fun to serious and not-so-serious situations also makes you a formidable force. In a recent study, it was found that people under 25 and women of all ages were determined to be the least humorous in our society. Yes, I know there is a desire for both of those groups to be taken seriously. The irony is if you take yourself less seriously, people take you more seriously.

The most important reason for being good-natured is that it allows you a gentle way to speak difficult truths. If you want to get away with saying what needs to be said, use fitting humor.

*"A sense of humor is not a luxury. It's a vital organ for survival."*

Seeing the funny side doesn't mean you have to tell and forward jokes or add a smiley face to your e-mails. Nor is humor grandstanding and drawing attention to yourself. Humor is being human and personal. It:

- Shows insight into human nature
- Makes life and work more pleasant for you and others
- Creates a relaxed, friendly environment; encourages others to do the same
- Is a great equalizer across barriers of titles, positions, and roles
- Increases your likeability and improves your connections
- Saves time in developing affinity
- Mitigates frustration
- Diffuses emotion
- Improves morale
- Lowers blood pressure—yours and that of others you work with

*"Laughter gives you an instant vacation."*

You have to make sure your humor fits. Choose the right time and place to use suitable, relevant, and brief wittiness. Still, if in doubt, go for it. Good people will be grateful for your attempt to put them at ease.

To ratchet up your quick wit: do or say something unexpected, present a paradox, give an anecdote, offer an odd fact or outlandish detail, or simply cleverly arrange your words to offer a surprise. One business journal writer took the slogan "What happens in Vegas stays in Vegas" and cleverly titled his blog post, "What Happens in Vagueness Stays in Vagueness." That's good humor. And limit your use of sarcastic, corny, or slapstick humor.

Light self-deprecating humor is good because it doesn't offend anyone. It's also an offensive move because it prevents other people from throwing the first punch at you. However, deprecating yourself is okay, but deprecating others is never okay. Also, don't overdo your self-deprecating remarks; too many may make it seem as though you have low self-esteem or other undesirable traits.

Yes, there is a risk in using humor as there is in everything else. Every once in a while your attempt at levity will fall flat. Sometimes you won't express the funny side well, or whomever you're speaking to will have their minds elsewhere and you are catching them off guard—or you are just not that amusing. Your attempt might have been esoteric, sardonic, sarcastic, mean, nasty, bizarre, or just not understood, and people will not laugh out loud. (I discuss how to apologize on page 132.) Do not let past misjudgments inhibit you from trying better the next time. Rethink your choice of levity, but do not stop the use of it. Your wit doesn't have to make others chortle nor does it have to generate the kind of laugh that makes people have to cross their legs, but it's good to at least cause a small smile. If you make your conversation or messages boring from a lack of good cheer, you will not be the first choice and you won't be taken as a serious and powerful contender.

One C-suite executive who lost favor with the CEO was described this way: "He talks too fast, doesn't smile enough, and has no sense of humor." Now there were other factors that led to his downfall, but that was the sentence said to the board. Sometimes being good-natured is more important than the right answer, decision, approach, look, or response.

### MAKE IT PERSONAL

People like to say that business isn't personal, but it is personal. All of life is people personally interacting with other people. Work is people interacting with people but with money and title attached to the interactions. Personal doesn't mean inappropriately intimate; you needn't border on sexting.

If you connect on a human level, you more quickly connect on a business one. How do you connect? Simply ask people about their interests, goals, and objectives; listen and remember what they said; later, bring it up. Connect human to human, not role to role, or gadget to gadget, or mano to monitor.

*Who, what, when, why,* and *how* are good words to use. Your tone must be one of honest interest and sincere inquisitiveness, not interrogation. Get to know the people behind the computers and the cell phones. Volunteer information about yourself as you ask about others. Then in every conversation, add a little bit more connection between you aside from the business purpose.

Find out, make note, and remember names of spouses, children, hobbies, and things going on in other people's lives. Remembering a small thing like a company anniversary, promotion, birthday, child's name, or interest will put you miles ahead of others. (Make note of my numerous references to questions throughout the book.)

Some hesitate to volunteer personal information, or they hang back when asked. They are not sure yet as to whether they can trust you. Over time they will learn they can. Even if they hesitate, inquire anyway. Give your own answer to the questions you ask of them even if they don't ask. Provide it nonetheless. You make it easy for them to get to know you and therefore to be more open with you.

We all think we're different, but there are more similarities than differences between us. What is most universal is most personal. Most people:

- Feel not fully understood
- Are the center of their own universe
- Want to see what they own go up in value all of the time
- Want to be appreciated, to feel powerful, and to appear clever or smart
- Want to be happy
- Want to make their children laugh
- Have a dark side, a part of them the world doesn't see
- In a time of trouble will assess their own exposure first, then gradually assess the implications for their friends, their town, the social fabric, and their country

*"Just like everyone else in the world, I am the smartest, have all the right answers, know what needs to be done, and am the best in the room . . . Oh, I almost forgot, I am the only one in the room!"*

The faster you get to contact people, connect with them, know them, and have an affinity with them, the faster you make an impact and difference. Humor helps.

### STAY FOCUSED

To stay focused on the phone, anchor your eyes on something. If you are talking face-to-face, you give eye contact, right? You center your attention on someone's face to have direct, level, straightforward eye contact to show and pay close attention.

On the phone, similarly, pick a focal point so you pay close attention to what is being said and help your mind wander less. Minimize distractions, and you will sound more engaging. Gaze outside your window, at a painting, a trinket on your desk, anything but your live computer monitor. However, it can be helpful to look at web pages that profile the person you are talking to. Look at a picture of the person if possible; some signatures include photos, and most social media sites also include photos.

Or close your eyes while talking on the phone. (*Obviously not while talking and driving!*) Closing your eyes takes away your sense of sight, but it ramps up your sense of hearing. You can shut out all that is going on around you and zero in on everything other people are saying.

Sit up straight, or, better yet, stand. Your voice volume improves because your breathing is less constricted. You think better on your feet.

Fact
♦ You speak, on the average, at the rate of 130 words per minute, but you listen, on the average, at the rate of 425 words per minute.

Hunched and bent over your computer hinders your tone of voice, spine, and general health. (*Note:* See page 85 on squaring your shoulders.) Talk to people as you would if you were face-to-face. First, it keeps you in practice for when you are talking to other people in person, and second, you sound better.

Slow down your verbal pacing on the phone, but keep your energy up. Speaking speedily makes you look nervous, preoccupied, impatient, busy, uninterested, or lacking in self-confidence. A fast talker is difficult for anyone to understand, in person or not. Then you have people who've worn ear buds too long and too loud and have poor hearing, people for whom English is a second language, older people with hearing loss, and ex-military people with damaged hearing. The list of possibilities goes on and on.

Refrain from trying to hurry the people along even if they are excruciatingly slow. Make supportive noises: "Hmmm . . . ah-ha . . . ." Don't interrupt their train of thought. Instead, jot down what you want to say and ask, but don't insert it until it's your turn to talk. Smoothly challenge the speakers if you do not like their direction, or ask them for clarification. Then allow them time to explain.

**ONLINE/OFFLINE: SLOW DOWN AND HAVE URGENT CALM;
DON'T BE QUICK, FAST, OR IN A HURRY**
Be unhurried (within reason, of course). Be markedly unrushed. Slow down when you talk, walk, respond, ask a question, enter a

room, shake hands, and leave a room. Be confident enough to take time. Move only when necessary.

*"Slow down. You'll go a lot faster."*

The more time you give yourself, the more status people will give you. Quick, jerky motions make you look nervous. Plus, when you talk and move fast, it's hard for people to absorb what you're saying. Pause as if you mean it. Don't let other people take you out of your calm. Talk at a slowed-down pace, but think fast. Be quiet so you can see and hear more.

*"Our CEO has a distinct sense of self-containment. He's never in a hurry, but he's still a beat faster than most people."*

Your composure will be contagious. People will ask you fewer questions and challenge or attack you less when you're calm and slowed down.

### SHUT UP AND LISTEN

When you're on the phone, speak when you have something to say; don't feel compelled to say a lot. Use fewer words than you are tempted to, and then stay silent longer. Don't fill awkward silences with chatter or always be the one to wrap up the conversation.

*"Say the right thing by not saying anything. Better to talk low, slow, and work out what you are going to say."*

Set yourself apart with your use of appropriate silence. That does not mean stonewalling, stalling, disproportionate stoicism, or stubbornness. It does mean using an on-purpose and for-a-purpose quiet. Your ability to pause will get the listeners' attention.

Be in a listen mode versus a broadcast mode online and off. Even when you are talking, use high quality listening by paying attention to the person's breathing, agreement or disagreement sounds, eagerness or lack of. You are rightfully taught early in your work life that you learn more (and usually earn more) with your mouth shut and ears and eyes open rather than the other way around.

Pay total attention to what is going on around you; try a forget-about-self approach on the phone and off.

> *"In a free society you have right to say whatever the heck you want, but that doesn't mean anyone has to pay attention."*

Listen for other people's intended feelings behind their words; encourage them to continue by saying "yes. . . uh-huh . . . go on . . . ." Don't disrupt their train of thought or discourage their participation by your interrupting them. When listening, do not simultaneously prepare your follow-up comments or retorts because you think you know what they are saying or they are going to say. Just pay attention. Do not hear only what you want to hear. Concentrate on what is actually being said. Every once in a while, shut up and listen up. Speak less, and have it mean more.

> *"My CEO rests his forehead on his intertwined fingers, holds the meaty part of his palms over his eyes, closes his eyes, opens them, and asks a question."*

### ANSWER YOUR PHONE

Have a nonirritating ring tone when receiving calls. Rap, cussing, train whistles, or Lady Gaga shouldn't be your first choice—better to be subtle, not bizarre. Be careful too in using the vibrate mode because a cell phone when it vibrates on some hard surfaces can sound like muffled flatulence.

Answer in as few rings as possible and with a pleasant sounding "Hello, this is Debra speaking. . . ," not a grunt (regardless of who caller ID shows is calling). Maybe your boss is borrowing the phone of a coworker you don't get along with. If you answer rudely because you expect the coworker, you'll have some explaining to do to your boss. Be consistent; everybody gets the same pass-the-salt tone.

The first thing to do when you pick up the phone is have a smile on your face, and maybe a corresponding twinkle in your eye. Callers can instantly hear a frown. If you can't convey pleasantness, or at least neutrality, why will anyone want to speak with you? Make callers feel comfortable, happy to speak with you, and glad they called.

### DON'T STARE AT YOUR PHONE

Don't gaze at, be buried in, or be glued to your cell phone as if your life depended on it. Smart people on smart phones can look dumb when they are so engrossed in their devices that they don't pay attention to anything or anyone around them. Unless you have a job for which you are on call (for example, you are a brain surgeon), you do not need to be staring at your phone all the time. Reholster it.

Besides, if you stare at it, you'll get BlackBerry neck: wrinkled from excessively bending your head down. It's costly to correct by plastic surgeons (I've checked into it!). Or worse, you could end up with chiropractic problems. Better to not bend your neck and spine.

*"When I see a person absorbed in his cell phone, sporting earbuds or a Bluetooth, I decide he's not worth a minute of my time."*

Ask before you pull your phone out at dinner. And don't hide it under the table, behind your menu, or inside your napkin to surreptitiously peek at it.

If you really want to impress the person across from you with the sincerity of your focusing your attention on him, take your phone out and, in front of him, remove the battery and lay the pieces lay on the table. (Actually, this step could also be helpful for your own security if you are having a highly confidential discussion. There is a cell phone program that allows your conversation to be heard by a third party if your phone is on, even if you aren't on the line. And as an aside, in general, remember that smart phones are computers, and if you have sensitive information on yours, it's absolutely necessary to have antivirus software to protect your data.)

Facts
▶ 28 percent of traffic accidents in this country are caused by people talking on the phone—some 1.4 million annually.
▶ The time it takes to type an average text while driving, you will have driven 300 yards—or three football fields.
▶ It takes 1.2 seconds of distraction to cause an automobile accident.

You can set the stage for answering an emergency phone call during a meal or a meeting with, "I'm expecting a call from my doctor/my boss/my son/my daughter/my dad/my mom," if it's true! A medical condition, fire, or an explosion is an emergency; a Twitter update is not.

Consider giving whomever you're with the present of staying off the phone! (As a survivor of a car that was totaled because the driver behind me was under the influence of his smart phone, I ask you to keep it in your pocket more.)

**ONLINE/OFFLINE: SAY YOUR "NO" ON THE PHONE OR IN PERSON; A "YES" CAN BE SAID ONLINE**

In a fast-paced workplace, it's easy to end up saying "yes" too quickly to doing something asked of you. Of course if the requested task is part of your job, the right answer is, "Yes, I can do that," or, even better, "Consider it done."

If it is something someone is asking or requesting of you that relieves him or her of work, you shouldn't be spending your time that way. If the action causes you to slight your own work, or it exceeds your grasp, you need to say "no."

When you say "no," be prompt, honest, and personal, but not pedantic. Briefly explain why you can't do what is being asked, but give an alternative to what you can do. Your alternative option lessons the hardness of "no," enables you to help where you can and how you choose to: "I can do (this) but I can't do (that)." Most of the time people ask of you because it suits their needs. They seldom consider your side, so you have to point out your situation to them.

*"My biggest mistake in life was not saying 'no.'"*

Depending on the situation, even if someone makes a request for you to do something that is not part of your job, that you don't want to do, that you are not sure you can do, or that someone else could do better, you might still choose to say "yes." You do not want to be viewed as a nonplayer. Give options, and set some boundaries or parameters for how, what, when, and why you'll do what you are committing to. "This is what is good, and this is what doesn't work for me . . . ."

Don't fear saying "no," even to your boss or boss's boss. Good bosses fear and hate sycophants. There are plenty of "yes" sayers in business—your boss needs a "no" sayer once in a while. If you have a solid, good reason for "no" with alternatives to help your boss get what he wants, you'll get more respect from him. I won't *guarantee* that your boss will be happy with you, but your approach will dampen the blow. If in haste or fear you say "yes" because it is easier at the moment, you may end up paying later for doing so.

*"For 20 years no one ever told the CEO 'no.'"*

Be able to say "no," but don't take "no" for the answer. First, understand that "no" is the standard answer or response from peers, bosses, and subordinates to test or challenge you, sometimes out of laziness, sometimes for reasons of budget and time. (Or they are doing it for the same legitimate reasons I suggested you should say "no.")

"No" is a complete sentence, but it isn't a complete answer. Don't take it as a matter of course if you believe that it could, or should, be otherwise.

"No" doesn't always mean "no," nor do *nada, nein, nyet,* not now, not ever, no way, negative, never ever, not as long as I live, over my dead body, not even if hell freezes over, not only no but hell no. More often than not it means, "maybe" or "I'm not sure." Unless you come back and fight for it, your opponents figured they were right.

So take "no" and go on. If you ask for something and are told "no," accept it; then ask for something different:

"Can you donate $500 million to the new college of business building?"

"No."

"Can you buy two tickets for the fundraiser next month?"

"Well, sure."

The above example is not "apples and apples," I know. Still, taking "no" is acceptable for some people, but it doesn't have to be for you. If you get "no," figure the person you are speaking with just didn't understand and you have to explain another way. My point is to keep trying, without being tedious, without just giving up. Ask 3 (or 13) times and in 3 (or 13) different ways before you even consider giving up. When people learn that you only redouble your efforts when you are told "no," you will get them trained to just saying "yes" right away.

### LEAVING A MESSAGE ON VOICE MAIL

Voice mail is a tool that lets people reach you when you're inaccessible, which helps you manage an influx of calls. You can count on the fact that many people use it to keep them from being interrupted. When you turn incoming calls into outgoing calls, you have time to prepare and plan for what you want to get out of or get across in the conversation. Listening to a message, deciding how to respond, then making the callback is more productive than answering a call and simply winging it.

The better the quality of the voice mail message that you leave on someone else's system, the better the chances are that it (and you) will be listened to. Frankly, people often don't listen to their voice mail messages. Or, if they do check them, they frequently don't listen to each entire message. Even your friends will tune out, fast-forward, ignore, and delete messages if you're tedious, dull, repetitive, and vacuous in your message or if they simply have lots of messages.

Facts
♦ 80 percent of time there is no need to speak directly to the person you're calling.
♦ 60 percent of respondents prefer leaving a voice mail message to leaving a message with an assistant. In other words, they prefer to rely on their own transmissions over those of third parties.

One woman rather proudly told me, "I keep my voice mail full so no one can leave another message. I love it when it's jam-packed. Then occasionally I just delete all." Still others devoutly listen to their voice mail messages even using software to transcribe them into a written form.

When you leave a voice mail message, everything we've discussed about preparation, pacing, intonation, and choice of words applies to that message. You need to think of leaving a voice mail message as being the same as talking live on the phone. In your message, you can make the most of your sincerity, passion, and enthusiasm to follow up, clarify, or reinforce a previous conversation or written message.

## BE PREPARED TO LEAVE A MESSAGE

When you initiate a call, always be prepared to leave a message so you are not at a loss for words if someone does not pick up on the other end. The following information should be on your mind in case you need to leave a message:

- Who you are
- What you are calling about
- What you want the other person to do
- When you need the other person to get the task done
- How the other person can reach you

One person told me he always brushes his teeth before expecting to leave an important message because it makes him feel cleaner and it helps him talk in a concise manner.

*"I always have a script even if I don't follow it."*

### LEAVING A MESSAGE

Smile while you dial, and take a deep breath before you leave a message. After the tone, pause because it calms you down as well as the listener, and it helps you avoid nervous heavy breathing, which can be misinterpreted. Speak clearly, deliberately, precisely, but also easily. Don't pause so long that you waste the other person's time or cause him or her to think you didn't leave a message and thus hit delete.

You should start off with a brief verbal-handshake greeting—for example, "Good afternoon, Janine. This is Debra Benton. My phone number is . . . ."

Start your message with your name and phone number. Do not make the listener guess for even a millisecond as to who is calling. Leaving your phone number up front makes it easier for the recipient to capture the information without having to listen to your whole message again as well.

When you speak, end your sentences in a solid, clear, and even a slightly louder tone. Don't let them trail off. Keep in mind that there is a chance the listener has poor hearing, has background noise, or is multitasking while listening to your message, so do everything you can to make it unproblematic to hear. Remember, if what you say is worth hearing, say it in a manner that it gets easily heard.

Repeat your phone number at the end of your message as well. Give an alternative to return the call such as an e-mail or instant messaging address. Make it simple for someone to respond. End with a clear, "That's all. Good-bye." Be brief. Don't rattle on. Leave one topic, question, or issue; don't leave several.

Also, don't ask anybody to call you back unless it is an urgent situation. Instead of creating a request, demand, or obligation to return the call, frame your message such that it is in his self-interest to get back to you: "Joe, you wanted information on ____. I have it for you. But before I can send it to you, there is one piece that needs to be discussed on the phone."

Leave it open for the person to get back to you but avoid saying, "I look forward to hearing from you" or "Please return my call" or "I need to hear from you, so call me back."

**ONLINE/OFFLINE: YES, YOU DO HAVE TO TOUCH**

Appropriate physical contact is a human way to connect and bond. In person you start a lot of conversations with a handshake: a double hand clasp (both people place free left hand over the right hand), the elbow grab, upper arm grab, shoulder shake, and wraparound embrace. Or you may elect to fist bump, high five, bow, kiss, air kiss, pat on the back, or give a light punch on the arm. The purpose of whatever physical move you choose is to connect as you reach out and touch someone. All ages need touch. One child psychologist told me young people need "four hugs a day for survival, eight hugs for maintenance, and twelve hugs for growth."

Any body contact that is an interpersonal power play or is intended to coerce, manipulate, and maneuver toward unwanted sexual relations in business is off-putting, bad, and just wrong. But body contact that reassures, relaxes, comforts, lifts spirits, makes someone happy, and reduces anxiety and stress in the workplace is a good thing.

Regrettably, the workplace has become "touch phobic," meaning that the chances of being sued for sexual harassment have increased over the years, consequently reducing the amount of positive body contact allowed. Furthermore, even subtle physical contact is gone from our daily lives, having been replaced by automatic bank machines, vending machines, online shopping, Internet, e-mail, and voice mail. Online your choice of words and tone of voice have to create figurative and virtual equivalents. How, you ask?

When having a phone conversation or when leaving a voice mail message or writing an e-mail, *start* with something individual to the other party—reference his family, a mutual friend, hobbies or interests, or some accomplishment. That one-to-one personalization is akin to a connecting "touch," and it reduces the remoteness between you.

If there is an option to listen to the message you left, take the time to do it. Check out your own tone, speed, volume, and clarity, and re-record if necessary.

Do not be irritated if people do not respond to your message. Technology might have failed, and the person might not have received your message. Maybe someone else got it and erased it. Other possibilities exist: the recipient doesn't have the answer or the information to respond, doesn't want to get back to you, or maybe even dropped the phone in the toilet and *can't* get back to you. Appreciate the fact that your call isn't the only one the person received today. Your need isn't his responsibility. Still, if nothing happens with one try, try again a different and better way.

At some point you might want to say something like, "I don't want to bug you by repetitively leaving messages. I need to get this information by (time frame) to give to (name). Unless I hear differently, I'll go with (this)." And be sure to say the above with a small smile on your face and without an underlying irritation in your voice.

ONLINE/OFFLINE: INTERNATIONAL AND INTERCULTURAL COMMUNICATION

There is about a 100 percent possibility that in the course of your day you will be communicating digitally with someone from a different country who has had a different cultural upbringing and who speaks a different first language than you do.

My advice is that you learn to play the corporate game that you are in no matter what your cultural background. You do not have to compromise your beliefs, dismiss your culture, forget the hierarchical respect for authority you were taught, or ignore your training to date.

*"All people laugh in the same language."*

But if you're going to play football, wear football pads, cleats, and a helmet, and learn and follow the rules of the game. You might have been raised to be a great cricket player, but don't bring your shin guards and bats into a football game, expecting to be ready to play or even to be well received. You have to play the game you signed up for.

That being said, if you are one of the football players, you would be wise to be help the cricket player to quickly become well versed in the game and to make it easier for that player to become acclimated. You will be appreciated and rewarded. It is true what they say, "What goes around comes around."

*"I was with team members on a call today in which one person was in California and one was in Nepal, and I was in Washington, D.C. I've worked with these people for three years, and I've never met them."*

There are as many ways to behave toward and with people as there are countries on the earth. And even within each country, there are regional variations of the larger culture. You cannot cover every single base, but you can have an approach that works with every single constituent:

- Accept differences.
- Be respectful and extra polite in words and tone.
- Use an appropriate level of formal title: Dr., Professor, Mr., Mrs., Ms., Madame, Mssr., and so on.
- Use lots of "pleases" and "thank-yous."
- Don't be loud and pushy.
- Minimize being overly direct and abrupt.
- Use straightforward terminology, not big words.
- Slow down; speak up.

*"Say 'please' and 'thank you' in the other person's language. Even if your pronunciation is clumsy, people appreciate the effort."*

Intense accents can hinder understanding when people are speaking, in which case, in-person body language can aid in comprehension. But, as mentioned earlier, online you have language software to translate and minimize misinterpretation. Still confusion occurs every day.

A female engineer told me about getting an e-mail from an overseas counterpart. He wrote, "I don't know what you are good for." She said she was quite offended, but she politely e-mailed back telling him she would be phoning him. She asked him to rephrase his comment for her to better understand, and she learned he was saying that he didn't understand the measurement technique she was using.

*"Most cultures are more hierarchical than the United States. Thus people are less outspoken. Your manner must not ruffle feathers but at the same time it must assert your position in the hierarchy which, again, requires firm but polite."*

To overcome a language barrier, you may need to e-mail, phone, and then e-mail and phone again to confirm understanding all the way around. Don't accept that everything is clear even if someone says "yes." In many cultures that just means "Yes, go on" or "Yes, I'm listening" or "yes, keep explaining." It doesn't necessarily mean "Yes, I understand and will take necessary action to get it done."

Learn some of the other people's language, but also their mindset and culture: their country's current or past history, geography, politicians, or other information. You are practicing being more human and personal when you learn and reference something about the world the other people live in. Ask so you'll learn.

*"One guy on my team twitters in three different languages."*

Be a little more careful with words as they may have different shades of meaning: *minute* (my-noot) and *minute* (min-nut) are two of hundreds of words that can be confusing for people for whom English is a second language. China has five different pronunciations for one word, for example. Also be careful with idioms and humor that may not translate well.

Think through your phrasing. "You have not delivered this" is not as good as "I am still awaiting X outcome. I hope it is convenient for you." Don't ask, "Do you understand?" but rather, "What more do you need to know from me to go forward?" Ask, "Would you rephrase that?" instead of "What did you mean?"

Be sensitive to religious or cultural custom regarding the timing of your contact. In the Middle East your team member may take time to pray five times a day. For example, France has five national holidays in the month of May alone.

Unless you lived in, have studied, or have been indoctrinated into another country's culture, you wouldn't know the nuances in their communications. The best remedy for understanding is to ask.

### RECORDING YOUR OWN VOICE MAIL MESSAGE

Many of us hesitate to record the outgoing message on our voice mail and rely on the computer-generated version instead. We leave the preprogrammed message on our phone because we don't like the sound of our voice (true for most of us) or we are lazy. Creating your own message, however, is better than using the automated one that depersonalizes the interaction.

Before you plan your outgoing message, call around to friends, offices, and people you admire, and pay attention to their recording. If a person actually answers, you can honestly explain, "I wanted to hear how you handle your voice mail."

If you hear a message that strikes you positively, jot it down; it may be something you want to use. Obviously, pay attention to what comes across poorly so you don't do that.

Write a short and simple script, and read it out loud to hear how it sounds to your own ears. If you like it, it's time to try your own. Stand up, square your shoulders, and, instead of bending over, raise the phone to your mouth level so as not to restrict the volume or projection of your voice. Smile, lower your tone, slow down, imagine someone in front of you (or get a friend to stand in front of you), and with calm intensity, purposefully speak your script.

In your recording, do not say, "I'll call you immediately" or "I'll call you right back" unless you *really* will. It is a lie if you don't. "I will call you back" will suffice, but say that only if you will call the person back. If you do not intend to return calls, don't say you will. Underpromise and overdeliver in what you'll do.

A female CEO I call has a friendly tone of voice with her simple message, "You know what to do and when to do it." Brief doesn't have to mean brusque; the plainness makes the caller feel smart versus dumb. The alternatives—"At the sound of the tone, slowly leave your name and phone number twice and time you called"—are boring.

One woman I know spells out "to—speak—slowly—and—clearly—when—leaving—a—message." Nothing overly wrong with that, but she could humanize it a bit more with "because what you are saying is important to me and I don't want to miss any of it." That takes a little edge off of the instructional nature and makes the caller feel his or her message is important to her.

One friend of mine has a one-word outgoing cell phone message: "Curt." That's all; not one more word. His name is Curt so he lets you know that you reached the right person. When I asked him about it, I kidded him with, "You know, 'Curt' as your message sounds a little curt." He laughed aloud and said, "Oh, does it?" He knows exactly what he's doing and does it with good humor. He added, "Maybe that's why people leave me such brief messages," which is exactly what he wants anyway.

(He is also the CEO of his own company so he has a little more idiosyncratic latitude than most.)

### BE BRIEF

Be briefer than brief in your outgoing message. It is irritation for the caller if you give the origin of your company name, your elevator speech, today's weather forecast, your website for the caller to go to, a list of multiple phone numbers where you can be reached, and the title of your latest blog post. Oh, and do not sing your message either. One person told me about a friend's message: "She always sings a short song in relation to what's going on in her life or of the season—spring, summer, fall." Even Jennifer Hudson shouldn't do that.

It's unnecessary to change your message every day or every time you leave the workplace. That makes it look like you have little else to do.

A humorous outgoing message is funny, but only once: "Hello, I'm available right now but cannot find the phone. Please leave a message, and I will call you when I find my phone."

A headhunter told me about calling a job candidate whose phone message was, "What up b-i-a-tch what you want?" The headhunter told me, "All I could think of was, 'I want nothing from you.'"

The goal of an outgoing voice mail message is to make it easy on the caller. A little lengthy, but full of information, example is this one: "I check my messages twice a day. If I don't get back to you within 24 hours, please contact my assistant. Alternatively, you can e-mail me at (address). I return calls from 2 to 4 CST. If that is convenient for you, I will try reaching you during that time." Although that message is somewhat long, it is helpful. (*Note:* If you commit to returning calls from 2 to 4 CST, you better do it.)

Experiment with speed, volume, variation of inflection, and

phrasing. Your tone and tempo sometimes convey more than the words themselves.

### DOUBLE-CHECK

After recording your outgoing message, call yourself to check how it comes across. If you didn't know the person in the outgoing message, how would you react? Because that's exactly what people are doing: sizing you up from one dimension. One person told me, "I thought I was giving a positive inflection, but when I listened to it, I was surprised how dully monotone I sounded."

Another who listened to her own outgoing message was surprised to learn the tone cue to leave a message was after an excruciatingly lengthy pause. She told me, "I finally figured out why I missed half of people's messages. They mistakenly started talking before the tone because it was so awkwardly long."

### ORGANIZING VOICE CONFERENCE CALLS

Telephone conference calls are just regular telephone conversations with a multiplying factor. Any advantage (or disadvantage) to using a phone call is magnified by the number of people on the conference call. Everything I've suggested regarding speaking voice, facial expression, and so on holds true. Number one rule: As the arranger of the telephone conference, you have to be comfortable and relaxed to help others feel the same.

As the arranger, cut others slack; cut yourself less. Naturally, it's unnerving for individuals to talk with other people they cannot see, so you have to adjust your attitude and prepare. Think through the issues, questions, and answers you will contribute. Then plan the tempo and tone. You want to duplicate the ease, comfort, and openness of a group of acquaintances sitting around and talking—all with keen interest on the same subject.

*"The number of people on the call multiplies whatever good you do; similarly, whatever you do poorly swells by the number of people plus 10 of each of their friends."*

### START THE MEETING

When scheduling the call, take into account the different time zones of the participants. Be sure that all of them are available to join at the scheduled time. Make sure they know how to utilize the technology at hand. If you are new to the device, practice using it before the call—not during it.

Send an e-mail agenda so participants can better prepare themselves. People will be more receptive and confident if they know what to expect and can plan how they will contribute. Then stick to the agenda. Don't surprise them with something that leaves them ill equipped to add value. If possible and considering the number of people participating and the available technology, share photos of everyone involved so as to put a face with a voice. Also, don't squeeze multiple objectives into a single phone meeting; keep to two or three at most. Save the rest for the next conference call.

Start the meeting on time; do not wait for latecomers, even if they are senior members. The moment you log into the call, assume the microphone is on and live to other locations, and be careful not to broadcast something you didn't intend to.

If people are joining in before the scheduled time, feel free to banter about the weekend football game, weather, or Tony Awards. If the small talk evolves into the purpose of the conference call, once everyone is on the line, add that information into your introduction so no one misses out on something important said before all joined in. It's your job to ensure participation from one and all. It's good to have everybody say something as the voice conference starts so that everyone's inhibitions to speak are lowered. This also gives you an opportunity to test the electronic workings.

Set ground rules: "I will frequently, individually engage with each of you by asking your opinion and maybe even poll everyone before going on to the next topic. This is to ensure that all participants get to be heard and to contribute their opinions, which can then be considered by everyone else."

Adhere to the agenda, and don't get derailed. You don't want people texting each other with, "Why are we wasting our time on this?" Just as you would in a live meeting, take breaks, or the participants will initiate them on their own. A half-hour is max to be on the call without a five-minute breather. Keep in mind that in some European cities that five-minute break may include a glass of wine so you might want to weigh the number of breaks you give and instead schedule shorter, more frequent conference calls.

Remember, this call is a meeting, so you need to give the same full attention to people as you would in person. You may think that since they can't see you, they won't know if you're focusing on the discussion or not. If so, you're inaccurate. People can sense your level of attention.

So even though they can't see you, behave as if they can. Stand or sit up straight, and focus your eyes on the shared documents, not on your personal text messages. Maintain a relaxed small smile; gesticulate to energize yourself and others on the call. Anything negative in your voice (talking too fast, fumbling, mumbling, using a nasal or whiny voice) will be exaggerated in an audio conference call.

*"Ask questions before changing topics and after making assignments."*

Prepare some stories to illustrate your points.

**ONLINE/OFFLINE: STORIES HELP PEOPLE REMEMBER YOU—**
**AND FOR THE RIGHT REASONS**

Explain and support your position with a story, anecdote, analogy, example, or a simple relating of personal experience. Coherent, compelling stories balance emotion with evidence. Make the narrative relevant and relatable; be explicit and implicit. A story can rein in your thoughts, keep the communication on track, and prevent you from getting flustered or lost and from wandering away from the main point.

When you demonstrate with a sequence of events, you hold the participants' attention longer so they get your meaning sooner. What you say or write in a storyline helps them better understand what you are trying to get across and remember it for a longer period. If there is humor in your narrative, that's all the better.

Sometimes a story is the best way to say what's on your mind without attacking. You are more interesting and more entertaining, and you can break through boundaries caused by diverse cultures and language.

Be anecdotal, and use examples: "Let me tell you about a situation I've experienced . . . ." Then add: "This is why it is important" or "Here's what I've learned from this" or "This is what it means to you" or "Here are the consequences . . . ." A survival story is the favorite for most people; explain how you overcame a setback or problem.

To be organized and keep from rambling, plan your stories with a beginning, middle, and end:

**Beginning:** Set the scene so that people get the context.

**Middle:** Explain what you did, especially where there were conflicts or complications and you did something others didn't.

**End:** Describe the outcome—that is, how it was resolved.

Maintain a running log of stories that illustrate the points important to you. A good rule of thumb is to have three stories for every important issue you deal with so you can pick the most suitable one while avoiding repeating yourself. An overused or overrepeated story loses its punch.

Now, before you read further, think about some of your own experiences that could translate into an appropriate three-part tale.

An example: Many people tell me they work well with others. That's important. But saying it that way is a claim and platitude. It would be much more believable, memorable, and repeatable if you said it in story form. Even better, instead of stating, "I'm good at working with people," attribute your accomplishment to someone else's saying it.

For example, if I claim, "I give really good career advice," my statement doesn't have a lot of strength. But if I say, "Client companies, like Kraft, Lockheed Martin, United Airlines, Verizon, and AT&T, think I give their people good career advice," that has a lot more power.

A story can go like this:

**Beginning (set the scene):** "My boss will tell you that I'm good with handling people. When I joined the company, I inherited a dysfunctional team."

**Middle (explain what you did):** "So I decided to spend one-on-one time with each member and try to find out what he or she wanted or didn't want and liked or disliked about the team and the current projects. All of the team members ended up telling me essentially the same things but in different words."

**End (describe the outcome):** "So I brought them all together and reported on my findings. There was some nervous laughter as I reminded them of things they had said and felt. From that day on, we were the most productive team in the organization, and we even won a company productivity award. That's one example of why my boss would say that I'm good at working with people."

Write your narrative down in detail. Use all the senses to paint a colorful and full picture. Now condense your story, and use more of a long sound-bite span when talking about yourself, your work, your team, and your project. Use the story in a telephone conference, a job interview, a job performance meeting, on a date, and with friends.

If you don't think of your experiences and formulate them into a narrative in advance of your need for them, you won't have them at your disposal when you want to call upon them.

Once you have these stories written down and condensed, literally sketch them out. You can create a stick drawing that only you need to understand, to illustrate the beginning, middle, and end steps. Your sketch will help you remember the account and tell it more smoothly, and it will be more memorable because you have it in your head verbally and visually.

### BE CONCISE

Set an example in being concise and to the point; in-depth follow-up discussions can be accomplished offline. Keep the conversation going; do not let lulls arise except for genuine contemplation time. One man, pausing, wisely explains, "The silence you hear is me thinking, filing, digesting what you are saying. Give me a minute to respond."

When talking, use proper sentence structure. Speak slowly and purposefully while clearly projecting your voice. Ask more questions than you would in person, especially to clarify for yourself as well as everyone else who may not be asking the questions but should. "What I heard you say was . . ." or "Am I expressing that accurately?" or "Did I miss something?"

Depending on the number of participants, have the individuals introduce themselves when speaking up. Instruct them: "When you contribute a comment, preface it with, 'Rock here' first."

It's confusing for other participants if people don't identify themselves. Be sure to set the example by doing that yourself; do not think you are the exception to the rule because you called the meeting. If people forget to say their name, chime in when they are finished and add, "Rock, that's a good explanation . . ." to identify them. It helps people who are taking notes to have the speakers differentiated, and it helps the participants know whom to follow up with later if necessary.

Treat everyone the same. Do not give more time, more compliments, more attention, or more questions to one individual over the others. Instead, spread your attention around evenly. Everyone gets friendly treatment but not overly buddy-buddy.

Organize what you need to do and how you plan to get it done from the beginning to the end. Don't cross your fingers and say a prayer. Plan it. Think all the way through, and write down an opening and closing remark or two along with no more than three points you want to make in the middle. Three max; at four you've lost them. Know your audience: who they are, what they want, their likely objections, and the potential obstacles you'll encounter. Prepare what you want to say and how; then do a run-through, at least in your head.

### FACILITATE PARTICIPATION

As the organizer, call on people who aren't speaking up, and say something like, "Emma, you had an interesting insight last week on ____. Would you share that with the group?" You don't want to put her on the spot, so by helping her remember something she knows—"insight you had last week on . . ."—she'll speak up more confidently. If you know you will be doing this routinely, you can send an e-mail or voice mail to individuals in advance saying that you will be calling on them to talk about topics of interest to both of you.

Little is understood, aligned, moved forward, or done unless the participants participate. If people don't come forward in the conversation, take a poll. Be respectful to the team members, but do not let them get away with not chipping in on the conference call.

*"I stay in the background and try not to be obscene or heard."*

When you are leading a conference call and someone asks a question, ensure that other people respond. Be quiet and wait until others insert a reaction. If necessary, ask for clarification to make sure that people are on target and in fact answering the right question. If you are the one posing questions, be ready to reword to clarify understanding for the group. Take responsibility for a lack of clarity; never blame others for not understanding what you are explaining.

When possible and fitting, refer to a prior conversation to show you listened and remember. Rephrase and repeat back what was said. The simple step of repetition or referencing what people have said makes people feel relevant. A side benefit is they note your potent memory and are more careful in what they say. The simplest statement that shows approval of another's idea: "To Sandra's point, I only add" shows that you're listening, concur, and can share your ideas without taking away from her.

*"I listen quickly and long."*

Don't jump in the conversation, bursting to get something out. Don't speak over others' words. Do not interrupt even if you need something to be made clear. Instead, keep listening but make a note so you can bring it up later. If the opportunity passes to say what you need to say, you should follow up in an e-mail. Your patience for not barging in will be appreciated by all. When you interrupt even with good intent, it's as good as saying "Whatever is going on in *my* mind is far more important than yours." If you absolutely, positively, unconditionally have to interject, do it one time. Even then, sincerely apologize, briefly make your statement, apologize again, and then shut up no matter how difficult it is for you.

### KEEP YOUR HAND HOVERING OVER THE MUTE BUTTON

Be ready to unmute fast to minimize any delay that creates an awkward lull before your response. Some systems have up to a 15-second delay in transmission, which can make it sound as if you are interrupting and talking over another person.

Don't make distracting sounds, shout, interrupt, or cover the microphone with your hand or a piece of paper. Don't tap the microphone, move it around, or bang or tap on the table. All of these actions resonate poorly.

If you elect to mute all attendees and take questions or comments only via the chat box, you will cut down a lot of the energy. If you use a laptop to take notes, mute your sound so people don't hear the rattling of keys, doors opening and shutting, and paper rustling. If you need the mute off so as to engage, explain with some version of, "I'm taking notes so as not to miss anything. If the keyboard sound is intrusive, let me know."

State when you are muting the microphone because the other site may think you have an audio problem. Unmute, pause, and then speak. Do not speak *while* you unmute, and pause a few seconds first, or half of what you say will be missed.

Mute sneezing, coughing, gum chewing, coffee slurping, belching, walking in the wind, heavy breathing, carrying on a side conversation, and any other sound that will be magnified. Also, turn off the instant e-mail and text message notification so you are not distracted by the sound of constant pinging.

*"One of my colleagues didn't mute when she was calling from home, and we could hear her say to her child, 'Mommy's on a very important and serious phone call,' and the dog was barking the entire time. The child answered, 'Mommy, then you should learn to mute Duke (the dog).'"*

### DO NOT MULTITASK

Better not to multitask while on the audio conference call (yes, I know everyone does it, but it still doesn't make it right). You will miss some important nuance despite how talented you are at keeping several balls in the air. You may feel you can do it without diluting any of your effectiveness on the conference call, or you may think no one knows and if, worst case, you miss something, you can always get it through document sharing later. All I can say is, again, think of the Golden Online/Offline Rule: "Do unto others as you'd have them do unto you." If it's not what you'd do in person, you shouldn't do it online.

*"There was a group of us on a call, and all of a sudden someone flushed the toilet. One by one we piped up, 'That wasn't me,' 'Me either,' . . . ."*

Besides, you're incorrect if you think the other participants don't know you're doing three things at the same time because they can't see you. They hear and/or sense your lack of attention evidenced by the poor quality of your engagement.

*"I did three chats and two e-mail drafts and a little gossip on IM to be entertained while on a conference call, and they didn't know."*

One person told me, "On a business development call with several people over many different time zones, we all could clearly hear one participant making lunch because she hadn't hit the mute button. It was discourteous and humorous, and none of us told her we could hear until afterward. She was mortified, but it was too late." Be the kind of person who pays attention to what others are saying out of basic respect. And be the type of person who says the kinds of things that people don't want to multitask over.

End the telephone conference call on time with a clear thank-you, wrap-up, and explanation of the next step. Keep things brisk, quick, and then end. Follow up the conference call with agreed-upon next steps to participants. And when possible, try to meet face-to-face before the next audio conference.

**ONLINE/OFFLINE: ASK MORE QUESTIONS THAN YOU GET**

Questions are the basic research everyone needs to do concerning everything and everyone. You learn about your audience, customers, clients, competitors, bosses, and team members so that you know better how to deal with, handle, and speak with them. You are other oriented not self oriented. You don't have to agree with people, but you need to understand where they are coming from.

*"With questions you gain empathy. It's as if you're saying, 'Buddy, I understand you (or your situation), and I can put myself in your shoes.'"*

A politically correct way to "touch" someone is to ask questions that develop affinity. You don't bond with people when you tell them all that you know; you bond when you inquire about what they know. Simply be other focused instead of self focused. You need to understand what the other person says, wants, will do, and won't do. And for that information, you have to inquire.

A good conversation to most people is when they are doing most of the talking. So let them; encourage them with queries. It takes pressure off you to perform, you make other people feel important, and you learn something you likely wouldn't if you were the talker.

To stop yourself from overtalking, occasionally halt midsentence, midpresentation, mid–heat of the battle, and ask who, what, where, when, why, and how about whatever is being discussed. By doing this, you will:

- Show interest in others rather than come across as just trying to get what you want
- Flatter others, and maintain their self-esteem
- Distinguish yourself from the know-it-alls
- Find out what the other people care about, value, like, and dislike
- Get a more honest assessment of the situation
- Avoid jumping to conclusions and making false assumptions
- Help guide people to arrive at the answer you want
- Buy yourself time
- Handle surprise and attack by asking for clarification instead of jumping into a defensive mode
- Persuade better
- Reinforce, clarify, or correct what you think you know
- Test and verify what they know

When you ask, choose your words and tone carefully. To ask is not to interrogate. At the same time, volunteer information without being asked so it's not one way; keep a balance in the give-and-take. If you only ask, ask, ask—even with sincere inquisitiveness—it can be perceived as distrust. Purposely ask some questions for which you know the other people have good and ready answers. It makes them look smart and clever. "Ryan, you won the contract over three competitors. What do you think was the key?"

Even your comments can be framed in question forms. Instead of, "We need to complete the project by Tuesday," it's better to say, "We need to complete the project by Tuesday. What has to happen to meet that deadline? Whom should we approach? What will cause the biggest hurdle?"

Ask three times in three different ways so as not to be tedious and monotonous. You get deeper, truer answers from progressively querying.

> First time, "Craig, would you give me more insight into your position on . . .?"
>
> Second time, "Hmm, okay, I get that. What about this consideration?"
>
> Third time, "Hmmm, I'm following you, but I'm still not clear on . . ."

> or
>
> "Can you give me an example?"

> or
>
> "Sorry, I'm slow in getting this, but run it past me one more time."

> or
>
> "Give it to me in layman's terms."

Asking is not stonewalling, stalling, or avoiding, and it's not being slippery, intimidating, dominating, embarrassing, nosy, or verbally stalking. Questions are all about learning so that when you do speak up, you'll know enough to make what you say worth hearing.

"What questions do you have?" "What would you like me to review?" "What else can I do for you?" are the questions taught to doctors to make patients feel good about office visits. Good leaders ask all the questions; they do not provide all the answers. That isn't their job.

Sit quietly and attentively. Wait until everyone else is done babbling. Ask pertinent questions. Ask for any additional opinions or suggestions, and then make recommendations with your reasons to back up your viewpoint.

When one of your people asks you a question, a simple "Good question" is a well-received way to start your answer. Caution though: If you use that response in a group session, you end up having to say it to everyone's question or else the person who you *don't* say it to will conjecture, "Wasn't mine a good question?" With more than one person, just answer the question without the preface. If you accidentally catch yourself saying "Good question" to one, then you need to say to the next one, "Glad you brought that up," and to the next one, "That's a point I want to make sure everyone hears," and "Another good question."

*"A good formula is this: Ask + listen + act on, and then report back."*

Make no mistake, there are stupid questions. They are the ones you ask because you weren't listening to what someone said and you ask the same thing the person just covered. It's like the human resources person who asked in an interview, "What was your biggest accomplishment at XYZ?" The candidate gave some examples of accomplishments, but because the interviewer's mind was elsewhere, a few minutes later the interviewer asked, "What was your biggest accomplishment at XYZ?" It was a stupid question because the interviewer hadn't listened to the candidate's answer, much less listened to herself asking the question.

## PARTICIPATING IN VOICE CONFERENCE CALLS

In a conference call, whether you are a participant or the organizer, take responsibility for making it a worthwhile conversation for everyone involved. You have been included in a group conference call for one central purpose: to contribute. Every X amount of minutes, offer something worthwhile, ask a question, or at least give a listening noise such as "hmmm," "ahh," or "ah-ha," or make a comment such as "Good point," "Great work," or "Thank you."

### BE PREPARED AND CONTRIBUTE

Just as you have to be prepared as the organizer, you have to be prepared as the participant. Make sure to dial in on time, or a few minutes early, so you don't miss any preconference chatter. If you have a ten o'clock meeting in person, it's smart to be there at 9:55, right? Same goes for appointment conference meeting.

*"If you're late with a high-stakes individual, you're an idiot."*

Know how to use the equipment features. Make sure you have tested the technical equipment beforehand. On a group conference call, it's often difficult to hear anyone who isn't right next to the hub, for instance. You don't want people to sit through the meeting, then later, because they couldn't hear the discussion, have to call other participants to get the recap from them as to what was said.

Locate and know how to use your mute button before you need it. A good way to lose your job is to say something stupid, offensive, or libelous after you *thought* you had muted the sound. Understand, though, that if you do use a mute button, you do run the risk of appearing to tune out because some systems notify other call participants who's on mute. You also need to remember to take off the mute function before you speak. You saying something brilliant that no one else can hear makes you sound not so brilliant.

Be aware of your surroundings; control the background noise.

One man joined in a call sitting by the pool where everyone could hear water splashing and children screaming and laughing and yelling out "Marco Polo." Added to that, every time he shifted on the outdoor pool furniture (skin against synthetic material), it made a suspicious noise (if you get my drift), none of which went over very well.

Identify yourself when you talk. Contribute. Don't just sit, listen, and absorb. Yes, take in, that's important. But remember, you're on the call to provide value, so make sure the other participants know you are doing so: "Adil here. Tamika, that is an excellent point," lets people know who is saying what both for clarification and for credit. When you do speak up, smile, gesture, and say it the way you would if you were there facing the group. Use the same energy. Your voice should demonstrate everything your body would if you were live or on video. No humming, haa-ing, throat clearing, fidgeting. Just talk and answer directly, with an affirmative outlook.

**ONLINE/OFFLINE: BRING A HAPPY HEART AND JOYFUL SOUL TO WORK**

Your attitude is more important than your education, history, or company experience. In life there are few things you have control over; your perspective and attitude are two areas you do. You will do better in life if you choose a most-things-are-possible philosophy and if you are cheerful, optimistic, and positive in your thinking, looking, and acting. Work life is 10 percent about what happens to you and 90 percent about how you deal, react, respond, and view it. You have to start somewhere, so begin things with a bright end in mind.

If you lose control of your attitude while under pressure from others, you lose, period.

Avoid being around people who don't control their perspective because it's like a disease—it's contagious. (I considered stating "Only optimists can buy this book" as I saw one CEO tell his customers concerning his company's products, but then I thought,

"No, pessimists can buy it too, and maybe I can turn their thinking around.")

Don't accept perceptions given by others. You decide. Nothing in life is one way or the other; it's always your chosen perspective toward it. Nothing is inherently good or bad; it's your examination and point of view that makes it so. If you get fired tomorrow, is that bad? No! Not for your replacement. For him or her, it's a good thing. Your reality is based on your chosen perspective. Don't think, "Well, that's being naïve." No, that's being in charge of your life.

For example, a woman I know of tells of fulfilling her childhood dream of quitting corporate America and joining the circus. Four years later she found cleaning up after elephants, riding white horses in the spotlight, and traveling from city to city had become tedious, boring, and disenchanting. The circus didn't change; her attitude toward it is what changed.

Take falling in love. You meet someone new: "Oh, he's so kind, so smart, so funny, so . . . ." Then seven years later on the way to divorce court: "He's such a jerk, so mean, so dumb . . . ." He likely didn't change; your opinion toward him did.

If you "sing" at work, it shows in person and online. When you look, think, and act with deep cheerfulness, you:

- Lighten your and others' burdens
- Increase your physical, mental, and emotional energy
- Have a better chance of fighting off a cold
- Make experiences delightful
- Have more fun than pessimists
- Live longer
- Are remembered when you're gone

*"Every morning I wake up thinking something wonderful is going to happen to me today; and when it doesn't, which is often, I think, it will happen the next day."*

It's okay to wear an enthusiastic, positive attitude on your sleeve. That's a constructive and productive point of view when coupled with plans to make it happen. A positive, optimistic approach will improve the outcome of the conference call, even if you're the only one on the call who has one.

Yes, I know that life is one darn frequently negative thing after another. It isn't for sissies. However, you survive it by being emotionally resilient and limiting the negative things that you add to it. No doubt, there is a risk to your optimistic perspective; sometimes a naysayer is right. Still I would rather drive into my brain days of upbeat thoughts and actions than allow harmful, unhelpful, downbeat, and destructive thoughts to seep in.

Overly optimistic beats overly pessimistic any day.

*"I'm always positive; sometimes justifiably."*

So what if you follow unproductive allegiances too long just because you're an optimist? So what if you are broadly buoyant in an otherwise downer situation? Could you possibly make a bad situation worse by being negative, or might you start turning it around? Be a radical optimist. It spreads digitally. If you choose cranky, that spreads too.

People make way for someone who boldly pushes past their negativity. Just do it. A positive attitude will not solve all your problems, but as one client said, "A positive attitude will annoy enough people to make it worth it."

Take notes during the conference call so you can remember who said what and refer to what someone said later. These notes also help you focus, listen, and remember the major and minor takeaways. That is productive multitasking. As I mentioned earlier though, if the other participants can hear the keys clicking, explain why.

Do not hog the stage. Stop yourself from being first, overly forward, and fast to jump in. Don't interrupt unless it is absolutely critical for complete clarification, and even then know that it will be risky. If you must, to possibly smooth it over a little, say something like this: "Blake, I hate to break into the conversation, but I must correct one assumption that is being expressed. If I don't, it will hurt all of our chances of success." Then briefly make your point and end with saying, "Blake, again, I apologize for interrupting, but it was important to not let the misunderstanding continue. I hope you're okay with my insertion?" Your tone must be nonexcitable, and your words should be clear, pleasantly assertive, and said with a small smile on your face.

It can be tricky to decide when to "fight for the floor" or when to wait it out and have a one-to-one meeting instead. Weigh the potential risk against the benefit of "grabbing the mic" before you inject. If your contention should be heard and discussed by the entire group, make sure to speak up or later you'll likely be criticized for not bringing it up. If the opportunity passes before you can say something, follow up with an e-mail or voice mail: "Stephanie, when you were talking about so and so, I didn't get a chance to offer this bit of information."

Get periodic feedback during the conference call by asking questions. You don't get visual cues so you have no idea as to whether your fellow participants are lost, bored, or think something is funny. You have to inquire. Also, it causes the participants to limit their multitasking if they know they'll be called upon.

As mentioned before, refrain from multitasking yourself. If you are only heard and not seen, you are tempted to do something else. Control the urge; don't do it. Concentrate with effort on the multiple of people who are on the call. Can you visualize how unproductive the conference call will be if everyone is simultaneously doing something else? The argument you used with your parents in grade school, "everyone is doing it," didn't hold then and doesn't hold now. Better to focus on the thing at hand; it's smart to do less better.

> *"We had a new mom of twins on our team. It was pretty horrifying for her when I had to call and tell her we all could hear the pumping machine through the speakers."*

Follow up. Do what you said you'd do. That shows "I listen," which gets you invited into conversations that are more important.

Lastly, don't fall asleep and snore, at least without putting the mute button on.

---

**ONLINE/OFFLINE: TO PERSUADE, CONVINCE, INFLUENCE, AND CHANGE THEIR THINKING**

You can't influence or change people's positions until you understand their positions—that's the pervasive power of personal self-interest. Figure out what the other people want— because everybody wants something. You can do that only by asking and listening, not guessing and assuming. Continue to ask, and check in to make sure you are satisfying their objectives and objections.

Ask:

- What do you want to achieve? Anything else? Anything else? (Ask three times because, remember, people lie in their responses, or sometimes they are lazy.)
- What don't you want to change? Anything else? Hmm, tell me more.

- What do you want to avoid? What is your ultimate concern or fear? Is there anything else?
- Who has a part in this decision besides you?
- When will you decide?
- How will you make your mind up?
- What do you still need from me to help you choose?
- What have you budgeted for this?

By asking questions, you assist people in understanding their own position as well as helping you grasp it. Understate, don't overstate, things when you show them how you can help them get it. Overlay your knowledge of what they want with what you want.

To do that, you have to know your own position too. Answer those same questions yourself. Think about what you want; know the outcome you're looking for. Have the successful end in mind. Consider what would be an acceptable second and third "right result." While being flexible, you still need to know where you will stop—that is, the bottom line where you have to put the auction paddle down and walk out of the room.

Without these steps you make a wish, not a pitch.

By listening to them, they will more readily listen to you as you explain your ideas. Through questions and answers, you come together.

Verbal communication on steroids is video. That is your future whether you are comfortable with that or not, so let's talk about video in the next chapter.

### WHAT'S IRRITATING ABOUT CELL PHONES?

After polling hundreds of people, here is what they told me that irritates them.

When people:

- Such as my staff, coworkers, friends, or others feel I should be connected all the time
- Are multitasking, that is, driving while talking on their cell phones
- Use the phone in inappropriate places—during a church service such as a funeral on in other formal settings
- Talk loudly in public places such as when they speak loudly to compensate for bad reception—without consideration for others in their surroundings
- Leave their phone on the desk or dinner table as if they are expecting a call
- Constantly check for calls
- Call me when there is a lot of background noise such as when they are in traffic, walking downstairs, or on a stairmaster
- Drop calls because of bad signals—they have poor connections and their reception is fading in and out
- Stay on longer than three minutes
- Mumble or don't speak clearly
- Just start talking without asking if it's a good time to talk
- Talk on their cell phones while they are interacting with other people, for example, at the grocery store or in line at the bank
- Don't tell me that I am on speaker phone
- Talk but don't listen
- Answer a cell phone call during a meeting, conversation, or while they are driving with me
- Yell at other drivers or kids in the backseat when they are on the cell phone in their car
- Don't allow me time to respond when they've asked me a question
- When people talk over me
- Answer in a nasty tone if the call came at a bad time for

them without accepting the fact that they had left their phone on
- Make irritating sounds such as blowing their noise or clearing their throat
- Have loud ring tones
- Have long conversations in public areas
- When people go on and on in general
- When people start long conversations when saying good-bye
- Call me when they know I'll be in the car
- Talk socially to me for long periods without considering my limited phone minutes

### WHAT'S IRRITATING ABOUT VOICE MAIL?
When people:

- Are long-winded and rambling, and when they don't get to the point and end up using the whole time
- Leave messages over 30 seconds long
- Leave a long a message even when I have to call them back anyway
- Don't leave their name because they assume that I have caller ID or that my phone gives me their number
- Leave incomplete information or an otherwise unclear message
- Give me their phone number or other information too quickly so I don't have time to write it down
- Call back because they see my phone number but they didn't take time to listen to my message
- Leave the message "This is so and so, call me back" without saying why
- Leave the message "Returning your call, call me back," which then just continues back and forth

- Use lots of uhs, umhs, ahs, and so on
- Hang up loudly without leaving a message
- Speak too quietly to hear
- Send multiple messages
- Call to tell me "I sent you an e-mail" or "I sent you a text message"
- Leave a message when I'm on vacation and they know it
- Purposefully call and leave a message when they know I am not available because they are trying to avoid talking to me
- Call back immediately after leaving a message, hoping to trick me into picking up
- Don't greet me and just start talking

# CHAPTER 2

## Video Channels

Video is a solid substitute for being face-to-face when participants cannot meet in person. Client updates, presentations, interviews, business meetings, training sessions, and general conversations are measurably more effective with video over audio only.

Those who grumble about the virtualization and impersonalization of the workplace can jump on this technology. With video you get to see body language, facial expressions, attitudes, and people's comfort level—all of which you miss out on with oral or written communication alone. Plus you have the added advantage of not having to smell the cologne on the guy mentioned earlier. If you're uncomfortable with being on camera or threatened by it, you'll have to get over it.

Fact
♦ Written communication (e-mails and text messages) get 8 percent of the meaning across. With audio it is 37 percent. In person is roughly 80 percent. When video is used, it jumps to nearly 100 percent.

For good or bad, video is memorable. You've probably experienced or heard of situations similar to the following:

- The CEO of a company participating in a customer's videoconference watched one of his people sit slovenly in a messy space the whole time. When the CEO got off the call, he fired the guy on the spot explaining that as the CEO, he had been embarrassed as had the entire team.

- The boss herself was the one who mortified her team by laughing and talking with her counterpart while on camera but with the mute button on. She forgot others could see her since they could not hear her. She didn't get fired, but she sure set a demoralizing example to her people.
- The bank honcho who joined in on a video call with his team, and carelessly forgot he was live, picked up the newspaper and started reading while occasionally picking his nose. One of the conference participants had to phone the CEO's administrative assistant, have her go into the CEO's office, and suggest he might want to stop what he was doing.
- Then there is the manager in a training video who dropped his pen, bent over to pick it up, and mooned everyone watching.

Mistakes happen, but if videotaped, they happen over and over and over again, every time the video's replayed.

All those bad examples, however, are offset with good applications of video like the company CEOs who regularly video themselves answering questions from employees, giving updates on business initiatives, and saying thank-you to a team for a job well done; the experts who use video for training; the legal teams that explain liability; and the marketing people who demonstrate product use and distribute customer endorsements and testimonials.

Whether or not you are skilled in, or are at ease with, talking into a camera, you will have to become comfortable with doing so because video utilization will be expected of you in your leadership role. If you are uncomfortable and cannot present yourself well on camera, management will rightly figure you will not be effective in the virtual workplace and will therefore find someone else who is.

## VIDEO PREPARATION

You have to put more preparation and planning into a video presence than an in-person presence because anything videoed, regardless of the quality, is potentially out in the universe forever. It had better be good. On video, people scrutinize everything you do. In person, people might politely avert their eyes so as not to stare. When watching you on screen, however, people study, pore over, scrutinize, ogle, analyze, criticize, dissect, and judge everything you do—and then forward the video to a colleague to do the same.

*"I can't Skype until I get some Botox, have my roots done, and Photoshop my face on someone else's body."*

Before you click on the camera or join in a videoconference or virtual meeting of any kind, think through the ramifications of what's about to happen. Take at least a little time to create a positive impression and make the exchange productive for all. Outline your objective. Rehearse your points so that you can:

- Inform and "tell, not sell"
- Relate a compelling story
- Be exciting
- Be entertaining
- Talk *with* the viewers, not *at* them

With prethinking, at the very least you'll relax and show respect to others, but in addition, you'll minimize freezing, failing, or fumbling in front of the camera.

*"I breathe deeply because it helps me talk when my lungs are full of air. I suck my gut in, get on the balls of my feet even though I'm seated, and get ready to be fired at."*

If you're using Skype, which is cheap and easy, to see the grandbaby in Alaska, you may not need to consider finessing the picture. On the other hand, if you do not practice when it is not important for business reasons, you won't be skilled when it is. Besides, it seems ingenuous to me to be half-good for the people you love and fully good for people you work with.

A casual approach will result in video regrets. Even if it is meant for a small, targeted audience, count on the possibility of your video's going viral. A poor quality, inappropriate, misguided, emotion-laden record on the Internet is permanently there—sort of like a tattoo typo. In fact, the poorer the quality, the more likely a foe will jump on a chance to disperse it to the masses if he or she can make you look bad.

### TEST YOUR HARDWARE AND APPEARANCE

Purchase or get access to good hardware, and know how to use it. Just as you might invest in a quality suit, car, and jewelry, invest in quality equipment. Video transmission equipment that doesn't work well makes for a dim impression. Run through the technical equipment you will be using so you are not confused by the device. Test the microphone more than once.

> *"Make sure your technology is user friendly; if it's complicated, people won't use it."*

You need a network that supports the necessary bandwidth for smooth transmission, which usually means hardwired instead of wireless. For example, if you have a videoconference with people in Boston, San Francisco, London, and Moscow, the quality of the bandwidth is going to vary tremendously.

Test out how you appear on camera. Have a friend rehearse with you beforehand. Test your proximity to the camera and microphone to get the best quality picture and sound. You might find that if you push yourself back away from the monitor so you barely touch the keyboard, your face will be lean without distortion, but then you have to ratchet up the voice projection to be heard.

Test the lighting as to whether it's too bright or dim. Get comfortable with having some illumination shine straight onto your face. Do not have it behind you because if it is, the participants won't be able to see your facial expressions. Also avoid overhead lighting because it creates unflattering shadows that make you look tired and old.

Test closing the curtain or blinds both for a better quality picture and to minimize your eyes wandering around looking outside and distracted. Try out what it looks like when you move around while some cameras are following you.

Then make notes of your settings and arrangements for future use so you don't have to perform a trial run every time.

### STAGE YOUR BACKGROUND

Send the message you intend to send by starting with the surroundings. Choose the ambiance for the purpose you want and with awareness of the effect it will have on viewers (for example, memorable, impressive, credible, genuine, trusted, liked, cool, calm and collected, competent, confident, and comfortable). Start by eliminating anything distracting or irritating to the viewers.

Spend some time watching people present on YouTube, webcasts, and television talk shows. Pay attention to what they do well and not so well; emulate accordingly. (You will see a lot of what not to do on YouTube.)

Watch newscasts where people are interviewed in an office and model your surroundings after the good things you see. A professional setting is likely uncluttered with just a few symbolic items: the right books on the shelf, family photo with 2.2 kids and a dog, an American flag if it's a politician, and so forth. (You have my permission to have my book in your background!) You lying on your sofa or bed, even with the American flag in the background, however, probably isn't a good choice.

Change your visual background based on the purpose of the video. Think of a Hollywood soundstage: prop, lighting, and backdrop set changes can take the viewer from a street scene along the Seine in Paris to a war zone in Afghanistan to a back alley in Detroit. A soundstage is one space with lots of opportunity. Relatively speaking, you can take people different places too. You can similarly have a couple of different backgrounds for your own uses (maybe not to the extent of a Hollywood soundstage) to make the transmission visually more interesting.

Something for you to note: Watch politicians on television. While they face the camera, they almost always have people of various racial, social, and ethnic backgrounds standing behind them staring at their heads. Why? To make it look like these people "back them." You seldom see politicians facing the camera by themselves at a big event because they don't want to look like they are standing alone. Believe me, e-v-e-r-y-t-h-i-n-g you see politicians do on television is scripted and has a conscious or subliminal purpose. (I'm sorry to say I've coached some of them, so I know.)

At the very least, move the plant in the background aside or over your shoulder versus having it look like it is growing out of your head. Remove pictures from behind you that don't have nonglare glass because their reflection could be annoying for the viewers. Take away anything that looks like smoking paraphernalia, alcoholic beverage containers, weapons, or items of excessive religious or sexual orientation.

*"Sloppy, cutesy, overly personal is not good."*

Some of the things people have told me they've seen in the background: what appeared to be a dirty pair of boxer shorts hanging on a cabinet, a used cat litter box, and a bra draped over the back of a chair.

*"People just don't think. They don't realize that everyone else is looking at it—no, they are locked in staring at it."*

Less mess is better. If it is clean and free of muddle, it reflects on you positively, and if it's not, it signals a watch-out.

*"I can smell clutter. I will discount you fairly quickly if you work in a mess."*

Anticipate surrounding noise that interrupts like a dog's barking at the letter carrier, a baby's wailing, a lawn mower or leaf blower outside your window, and trains, planes, or automobiles going by. Situate your well-charged or plugged-in camera or laptop in a quiet room where people coming in and walking around, opening and closing doors, during the call won't disturb you. Turn off anything that rings, taps, beeps, glows, vibrates, or grabs your attention. Do what you can in advance to minimize and handle any sound surprise.

*"When my dog starts barking, I just say, 'He has an opinion on what we're talking about.'"*

Have a dress rehearsal. As it would in Hollywood, a theatrical dress rehearsal means a costume run-through, so plan your attire too. Put some effort into preparation regardless of whom you're talking to. If you consistently put best practices in place, even down to your outfit, you won't be caught off guard and unprepared when a critical video event happens.

If you are presenting a slide show or other documents, confirm with the host or your technology department that your versions are compatible with the those of the sharing platform—say Mac versus PC. Have the shared-document technology under control before you try it for the first time. Close the other programs. Have nothing confidential up.

A videoconference participant didn't turn off his IM chat, and someone in the room texted him, "Can you believe this buffoon," which popped up on the shared screen. Another good way to lose your job, especially if the buffoon is your boss. If you use document sharing, don't say the same information that's on the slide; use the slides to interestingly illustrate something you're saying, not just repeat information.

When you log on, you could do a short wave hello to identify yourself, especially in a group. Use other people's names in greeting. Since there is frequently a system delay, bring attention to yourself with a simple hand signal, or by asking "Questions or comments?" before you start speaking so the first few words don't get missed

If people join you in the space, check out things for them too. Don't set it up so that you come across better; that's just tacky (for example, don't use better lighting, sound, or backgrounds than you use for everyone else). Of course, there's no reason to see to it that they come across better than you either.

**ONLINE/OFFLINE: APPEARANCES MATTER**

Your visual presence sets the impression that you make before you have a chance to open your mouth and prove otherwise. Even then, the visual primarily wins out over the verbal.

By appearances, I am not referring to the latest Japanese camera that will whiten your teeth, remove dark circles under your eyes, shrink jowls, and retroactively apply makeup. The effort required to make a positive in-person or on-video impression is less than the effort required to undo an unfavorable one.

To make a constructive impact in person, you walk into someone's office wearing appropriate clothes with a relaxed expression on your face. With good posture and your eyes on the prey, you approach Mr. or Ms. Big and pause. You shake hands, and pause again. You pull up a chair, and with a continuous erect posture, you lower yourself to the edge of the chair. You ease toward the back, position your arms in a symmetrical position, and begin the conversation.

*"You have three seconds to establish your presence. Two seconds to size up the situation and how to approach it, and one second to correct yourself if you're wrong."*

On video, you're already there: front and center from the first second on. You don't get to make your entrance, so what they see in front of them better fit.

*"Get in, get it on, and get it done. I show up with nothing in my teeth, fresh breath, lipstick on, and shoes polished. No one smells my breath, but I do. No one sees my shoes, but I do. I'm ready for battle."*

Having been raised with television, we're very skilled at seeing a person and in the first five seconds sizing up—accurately or not—the person's likeability, social status, intelligence, competence, and success level. You do that to others; they do that to you.

*"We have no clue what we are looking for; we just know it when we see it."*

It may seem unfair that looks matter, but it is the currency of business. People who say they don't care about appearances are faking it—or are being disingenuous.

People believe what they see despite the fact that the opinionated size-up stems from a combination of stereotypes, what the media depicts, and past experiences. I heard one recruiter turn down a job candidate saying, "You can't trust a tanned man."

*"How you dress, sit, and talk tells me who you are."*

**CLOTHES DON'T MAKE YOU, BUT THEY CAN HINDER YOU.**
Your work is more important than your jacket and pants; you still need smarts or else you're just an idiot in a smart suit.

Just because people see only a half or quarter of your body on video doesn't mean you shouldn't be wearing full-on business or professional casual attire. People often end up seeing a lot more than you might think. When the ads say you can "go to the meeting in your pajamas," don't. Accidentally letting your business associates see your Sponge Bob pants when you stand to retrieve something isn't a good thing.

You can sway the effect you have on others just by your clothes. That's the fortunate reality if you choose to be mindful of details; it's the regrettable reality if you dismiss the importance of it.

*"I dress like a matador in preparation. I put on my lucky shoes, necklace, and ring."*

One lawyer wanting to appear "green" explained that he wore skinny ties for environmental reasons as the "thinner tie emits less carbon." The "right" dress code is the one that fits the environment you're in. Be *your appropriate* body, age, season, culture, country, industry, customer, or supplier, and then stick with it. Be consistent whether you're meeting with a man or a woman. Also, remember that just because a company has a relaxed dress code, that does not mean the business environment is easygoing—you will find you are mistaken if you think it does.

*"In Silicon Valley dress is so important that the buzz is that it isn't. We celebrate informality, and people like to act like they don't care about dress, but it's all about dress . . . They think, 'If we don't wear suits, we won't be suits.'"*

Still, I understand the desire to express one's individuality. Fine. Do it in your work contributions. Don't do it in your appearance alone. You can still be yourself. The dos and don'ts I write are not to suppress, repress, or take away your uniqueness. They are to keep you safe, focused, and rewarded for your efforts, not waylaid because of some eccentricity, carelessness, or casualness.

If you don't want to be told the size of your earrings, color of your belt, or height of your heels, skip this next section. But if you have some interest in what your bosses won't tell you because of its personal nature or legal implications, or they like keeping you in the dark—read on.

Regardless whether you are a man or a woman, pull your hair off your face and out of your eyes. Don't play or fiddle with it because doing so makes you look nervous and/or flirtatious.

On camera, try to avoid hat hair or bed hair; pump up your hair and touch up your makeup if you use it. A little lip and cheek color will suffice, and blot your nose and forehead to lessen the shine.

Ladies, online or offline, wear a jacket or vest over your dress, skirt, or pants instead of a clingy, soft dress alone. If the air-conditioner is on, keep the jacket on (if you get my meaning). Minimize overtly emphasizing your breasts, cleavage, or rear end. Your clothes shouldn't be more interesting than you are. Candidly, you can wear high, spiky heels if they won't be seen on the video, but why would you? Do remove the noisy bracelets, and keep the extreme dangly earrings for after work hours.

*"When you wear revealing clothes, I figure you have something to hide."*

I know talk-show personalities and actors playing lawyers or executives on television wear low-cut blouses and short tight skirts—the office cocktail dress. If you choose that attire, a lot of men will appreciate it and will look at you with a straight face as if they are talking and thinking about business while in fact they are pondering, "I wonder what she looks like naked."

I'm not saying this is fair; it is reality though.

Men, wear collared shirts. A crew neck can work with a sport or suit jacket, but it does not work as well alone. Striped or checkered shirts on either sex can cause a psychedelic pattern, particularly with any movement.

Have your clothes be fresh looking and not like you traversed the Himalayas in them. The unemployed car wash worker look is out as well as the t-shirts that read, "I'm with stupid." Have a reasonably groomed, not radical haircut; harvest your nose and ear hair and dandruff. Clean your finger nails *off* camera. High-definition cameras see every detail. A wrinkle in a shirt is exaggerated as is a five o'clock shadow. Keep a mirror nearby, and look at it before a video call.

Men, have an electric razor at your work desk so you can do a quick once-over before showtime. You can blot the shine off your nose and forehead—and fluff your hair too. Keep a spare jacket in your work space to slip over whatever you are wearing if a video call happens at the last minute.

Darker colors make you look thinner; cameras add 10 pounds. Don't wear orange because it looks like prison garb.

Again, be aware of your background: If you have dark walls, you want light colored clothes. With light walls, the darker color works for the contrast to better view you. Similarly, consider your skin tone and select a contrasting shade. Blonds get washed out with white walls, for example.

*"I consider every bit of even small criticism I might get: my dress, my hair, my jewelry—everything people might use to diminish what I'm presenting—and I go through it myself and correct it before they can attack it."*

Sport no visible tattoos (unless you're part of the Maori tribe) or viewable body piercing; ear lobes are okay but pass on nose, lip, and eyebrow. In spite of the fact that 40 percent of the population under age 35 has inked tattoos, keep yours under wraps at least initially. Check out the acceptability with your audience before you spring it on them. (See more on tattoos on page 86.)

Early in your career spiff it up a bit. Dress a little better than your peers or what is required. You can relax your dress code after you've achieved some success. Older boomers need to update their clothes a bit too or risk looking dowdy or as if "I am over giving a damn about appearance." Frumpy doesn't work for either end of the age spectrum.

Very seldom will anyone at work say something to you about the way you dress, despite how much it might bother them. They don't want to hurt your feelings; are embarrassed about commenting on something so insignificant as dress; fear some sexual harassment accusation in retaliation; or simply don't know what to recommend because they aren't sure for themselves. Because they don't say anything, you might not think anything is wrong, but you could be incorrect.

*"You don't want to be known as the girl with the belly button ring. You may have the greatest idea in the world, but if you are known as the girl with the belly button ring, you won't be taken seriously."*

Although I am for doing what others don't, dress is the exception. There is a uniform you expect to see on a car wash attendant, cowboy, courtesan, professor, lawyer, ambassador, or C-suite executive. As one man described work clothes, "It's simply office camouflage." If your choice is measurably off the mark from what the managers and executives wear in your company and industry, make note and change. Why let something so insignificant hinder your career progress?

Working remotely around the globe, videoconference calls can happen during all hours of the day. You want to look groomed, awake, alert, and alive at your end of the workday as the people joining in from different parts of the world do at the start of their workday.

*"I conference out of my home office on the weekends late at night*
*for the European time zones, but I still put on a suit jacket and tie.*
*They never see the boxer shorts, well, except for the one time I had to*
*stand up and get something and come back to the camera."*

One CEO told me about a video call with the U.K. oil minister and the U.S. ambassador. The CEO wore a tie showing King Kong climbing the Empire State Building and a British bowler hat. He thought it would get their attention, bring a little humor in, and it did. He carried it off with confidence and his powerful Australian accent. Something you can do too when you're meeting with the ambassador to England, but for now let's *not* have your clothes be your personality.

*"I put on a pair of eyeglasses because I read a study that said they*
*make you look smarter. They don't even have lenses in them. They're*
*just a frame."*

And yet, with all that I've just written, I want to emphasize that I'm more concerned about *how* you wear than what you wear.

**SQUARE YOUR SHOULDERS**

Square your shoulders; don't be round and hunched over. Keep your head straight, not tilted toward one side. We like "level-headed" executives—that being one of the physical descriptions we use in our language to describe character along with "can look you in the eye," "stands on his own two feet" as compared to being "spineless," "gutless," and so on.

You prevail if you sit or stand up straight, tall, and square-shouldered and you walk like a winner. You lose if you don't. If you look like the prey, someone will target you, and it will be your own fault.

*"It's not the load that breaks you down. It's the way you carry it."*

Most people lazily take on "the posture of a 50-pound potato sack that was only three quarters full" as one person described.

Force straightness into your spine. Get up against a wall and put your shoulders, rear, and heels against it. Stretch out your clavicle. Breathe. Now walk away keeping that posture: shoulders back, head up, chin level with the floor.

*"Fully occupy the space in which you find yourself."*

Move firmly and forcefully whether you are 18 or 80. Regain the posture you had as a six-year-old on the playground until you started carrying a heavy backpack, followed by a computer bag, diaper bag, and the weight of the world as an adult.

Observe others to emulate the ones whose posture comes from self-discipline. Look to those who seem to be constructed in straight lines and who move with purpose regardless of height.

*"To be well dressed, you must be well naked."*

More than one study has found people with better posture were more self-assured as opposed to those who slumped. Good posture improves your health, your voice, your appearance, the way your clothes hang on you, and your effect on others.

Bad posture conveys boredom and bad attitude. It makes you sound out of breath and look weak or tired and loser-like.

### REAL BRANDING: TATTOOS

The good news is that tattoos aren't reserved for criminals, sailors, social misfits, warriors, sideshow freaks, rock stars, and outcasts anymore. For these reasons and others, one in three people under 40 has at least one tattoo. (They are actually an ancient art form dating back to the Egyptians who used them to control the supernatural.)

In the future, younger executives will replace older ones, and the young ones will sport tattoos so it will become increasingly less of an issue in dress codes and social reactions. But today, a general rule of thumb is: If your boss's boss is showing his, you can too; if not, cover it.

*"Scars are tattoos with better stories."*

A mentor of mine used to say, "A tattoo is akin to wearing the same hairstyle for the rest of your life." That being said, if you have your reasons for getting one—to feel sexy, be rebellious, for sentiment, or because you belong to the Church of Body Modification—then put thought into the following:

- Try on a temporary tattoo as a test for a while.
- Select the spot on your body very carefully. Make sure people can't see them unless you want them to. Avoid locations that can't be concealed by normal dress; stay away from your neck, fingers, or hands.

- Think about where you see yourself in 10 years, and ask yourself if the tattoo fits in the picture. Consider that it will likely limit you in some jobs if it's visible. You may not as quickly get on the corporate fast track or be nominated for Supreme Court judge. Also, consider whom you'll be with. A friend had his girlfriend's name "Pat" tattooed on his forearm. When he ended up married to Teresa, he changed "Pat" to "Bad" because that was the best he and his artist could come up with!
- Ask yourself, "Is this a piece of art I'd like on my walls? If not, do I want it on my body?"
- Picture it on your mom and dad because one day you might be one and your kids will look at you the way you see your own parents.
- Quadruple-check the stencil the tattoo artist will use on you. Check for typos—"Angel" can easily come out "angle." Sanskrit characters you think say "stronger, higher, faster" might really be saying "I have three boobs."
- Think about the fact that the tattoo removal business is a growth industry—and I'm told it's 20 times more painful removing than getting. One man had his children go with him to witness the painful tattoo removal process in hopes to deter. A new establishment in my town to remove tattoos was interestingly named, "What Were You Inking?"
- Buy some tattoo concealing cream for emergencies.

*"Don't bring generously tattooed arms to the office."*

If you are around people who sport them, know that there is a requisite tattoo etiquette. Just smile and with respect say, "I like your tattoo" or "Tell me about your tattoo." Don't touch it (because that's sort of like patting a pregnant woman's stomach). And don't say:

- You're going to regret that in five years.
- That's ugly.
- Why would you do that to your body?
- What do your parents think?
- Is that a tramp stamp?
- Are you on drugs, or are you just stupid?
- I know someone who can remove that for you.

### GOING LIVE

Slow down when you go live. You want to appear calm, confident, and competent, so move unhurriedly as you push up your glasses, reach for a pen, gesture, or scratch your eyebrow. Fast moves make you look nervous, harried, or hurried, and they also put others on edge. Although you should avoid jerky, rapid movements, don't be dully stiff, rigid, or robotic either. Refrain from watching the webcam image of yourself too much. I've seen people continuously primp and adjust—which should have happened in the mirror beforehand.

*"I worked so hard to prepare that I was exhausted and presented in a quiet calm manner."*

Expect to be disappointed with your video outcome. Yes, I know you have a high standard for yourself, but do not expect to come across as well as what you see on television. You have to remember those people have:

- Professionally written scripts (even the ad lib banter)
- Hours spent on makeup and hair
- A stylist to select their clothes
- An image consultant to show them how to walk, talk, sit, pose, gesture, and move

- Professional directing and sound people
- Rehearsals
- Expert staging
- Professional-level cameras and lighting
- Numerous takes and retakes

A professional videographer told me that for a three-minute executive presentation, he shoots 7 to 17 hours of filming and that "tons of footage gets thrown away." His finished product has edited angle changes every three to four seconds.

He says that if he is filming the CEO, he shoots from a closer and slightly lower angle looking up at the CEO to make him look more powerful. If he films a junior person, he will film further away, from a higher angle looking down, and often over the shoulder. "I'll include a little of the CEO's shoulder in the shot as if to show that the person is the CEO's shadow."

Typically you're not going through that much effort on a video call, but keep in mind that static visual imagery quickly becomes uninteresting to today's brain trained to (1) see scene changes every three to four seconds like on TV and (2) view interactive websites where people read left to right and top to bottom as their eyes move around the page looking for icons, links, hyperlinks, and so on.

Fact
◗ A 30-minute television show will have upward of 2,200 angle changes.

I am not suggesting that you shift your body, move your head, and change your background every three to four seconds—such excessive movement would be distracting. However, if you want to keep people interested, I suggest performing purposeful periodic movement that fits what you are saying.

Fortunately (or unfortunately), the proliferation of amateur YouTube videos has lowered our standard of video excellence expectations. That being said, since most anything online will be around forever, strive to make yours the best quality possible.

(I let a young videographer practice on me. The low-cost production ended up on YouTube, and there I am in all my glory, totally green—hair, skin, clothes—and I've yet to be successful in getting it removed!)

Spice up your video transmission a little. Using a prop, even some random silly, gimmicky stuff once in a while, will grab attention and curiosity as the viewers think, "What will he be doing with that?" Even hand-drawn charts, à la those of the political pundits on election night, are a break from PowerPoint slides.

Arrange a chair so you can sit with your upper body resting asymmetrically—one arm away from your body on an armrest, the back of the chair, or a side table. Sitting with both arms and hands doing the same thing—symmetrically—makes you look tense. Watch the morning talk-show hosts and how they sit and push their arms away from their body. Seldom will both arms and hands be doing the same thing because it looks tense and uptight. In fact, try standing rather than sitting (the camera has to adjust, of course).

Practice your gesturing too. Better to go to the side rather than in front of your body while still staying in the picture frame. You don't want to stick what comes across as a gigantic finger in the viewer's face when you flail it in front of the camera. Gestures paint a picture to illustrate your point and make what you say and how you say something more interesting and memorable. Move and gesticulate purposefully, to help paint a picture, but don't wail and flail your hands either.

In a videoconference with other people in the room, a judicious placing of your hand on the shoulder of the person next to you as you introduce him or her adds a dimension of connection to the viewers.

Turn your hand sideways, not sprawled out flat facing the camera, to make your gestures look smooth and supportive as compared to contrived, and gesture simultaneously to your corroborating statement. For example, if you say, "Any questions?" raise your hand (which is the generally accepted body language for asking a question) before you actually say the words. If you say "Any questions?" and then raise your hand after asking, you look stiff and awkward.

Take a drink from a coffee mug the way you see the guests on talk shows do. This action makes you look relaxed and gives you something to do with their hands. Be careful that it doesn't go down the wrong part of your throat so you start coughing. Also avoid milk or dairy drinks because it clogs up the throat (well, you should probably avoid tequila also which may loosen your throat a bit too much).

Present yourself as if you are in person with just a tad in excess of what is required.

> "Sometimes for emphasis I pound my fist on the table, which jostles the computer a little. I've even grabbed a hold of the camera and shaken it a little as I've asked, 'Can you see my frustration?' It sort of looks like an earthquake on their end, and it certainly gets their attention."

**ONLINE/OFFLINE: KEEP YOUR EYES ON THE PREY**

When presenting in person, it's best if you look directly at one audience member and speak to him for the duration of a sentence, a thought, or a phrase. Then pick out a different person to give the same focused eye contact. Going to different parts of the audience with one-to-one eye contact looks better to the audience than if you try to scan the whole room and give a fleeting glance as your head wanders back and forth over everyone.

It's a little counterintuitive because it seems like you should include everyone, but you actually look scattered, nervous, or shifty while scanning the crowd. And an added benefit of a steady focus on one person is that it minimizes distractions.

When making eye contact, a good action is a visual pause: slow down, and with a level head, look over the person's shoulder and halt briefly. Try to avoid looking up with your eyes toward the ceiling or down to the floor. Roving makes you look scared, scattered, searching for your thoughts. Then look back to the person, and with a relaxed facial expression and calm voice, continue. That pregnant pause relaxes you, gives you a second to gather your thoughts, and makes whatever you say next sound especially significant. Strenuous furrowing of your eyebrows and forehead does not make you powerful, influential, or appear to be listening carefully. It looks like you are furrowing your eyebrows.

Don't have shifty eyes, and don't fidget, frown, chew your lip, gnash your teeth, brush phantom strands of hair out of your eyes, or nod your head like a bobble-head doll. Instead of a jerky head gesture, try one slow, deep purposeful nod.

Maintain eye contact by looking into the camera. One person drew a set of eyes around the camera and added some fake eye lashes to give better eye contact. If you use a teleprompter, keep it camera-eye-level.

Eye contact on camera is to the camera, not the person on the monitor. (If you do look at the person on the monitor, remember to look at the top of his or her head so you won't have half-lidded, half-droopy, sleepy-looking eyes.) You don't have to stare at the camera only; just as you look over someone's shoulder in person, you can look over the camera's "shoulder" to break the gaze. A good idea is to lower the monitor camera a little so you don't have to look up at it.

When a person on the videoconference call who is in the same room as you asks a question, you can answer looking at the person. If someone asks you from a remote location, answer to the camera. Ironically you actually get more eye contact on camera than in person today. If you're talking to a group, you are likely looking at a room full of laptops staring back at you.

> It's a given that this will be uncomfortable at first. That is irrelevant; my interest is in the positive impact and impression you make when you do it well.

## SOME VIDEO DON'TS

Don't surprise people by videotaping them without their knowledge. Also, do not engage video chat without the other person's permission. Most computers have cameras, and bosses have been known to disengage the automated message, "Christopher is requesting a video chat. Do you accept?"

Mary moved into her new home about the same time her remote boss had updated the computer systems. Hers was set up in the bedroom while a few renovations were being finished in her home office. "Good morning, Mary. What do you think of the new system?" texted her boss.

"Really puts us on the cutting edge. I'm excited to learn more about it," she answered.

"You'll pick it up quickly. By the way, I like your new haircut."

"What did you say?"

"Your haircut fits you well."

"You can see me?"

"Yes, isn't it great?"

"Uh, not sure," she said, as she quickly stuck a her hand over the camera as her husband, stepping out of the shower, naked, walked behind her. Accidentally, or on purpose, the default settings had video chat come up automatically without asking her in advance. Had he gotten out one minute earlier, the boss would have gotten a full frontal introduction to her husband.

Here's a brief list of some video don'ts that you should always keep in mind:

- Don't walk and talk on video even though you can with a mobile device; it's off-putting. Nor should you have a video chat on the go no matter how edgy it appears. Plan a time when you are not in motion.
- Don't play with things: eyeglasses, pens, buttons, hair. Don't doodle, fidget, or yawn.
- Don't touch yourself in a self-comforting way (stroking your hair, chin, or other body parts) because psychologists say it suggests you'd liked to be touched there by someone else.
- Don't eat, smoke, or glance at your watch.
- Don't have an ashtray with hand-rolled cigarettes in .the picture.
- Don't perform body maintenance: floss, clip toenails, paint fingernails, or use a toothpick.
- Don't take a nap.
- Don't drink from anything that resembles a shot, martini, high-ball glass, or beer mug.
- Don't wear sunglasses.
- Don't look bored or irritated even if you are. Maintain a delighted look on your face.

Never forget that you're being watched—in fact more so than if you were in person. Remember, in-person politeness forces people not to stare, but on video there are no such restraints.

---

**OFFLINE/OFFLINE: CREATE CONFIDENCE AND COMPETENCE IN OTHERS**

You have to excel as an individual contributor but also raise the team with every communication channel that you use. A boss asks himself or herself two questions when hiring: (1) How will this person perform the job? (2) How will this person affect others?

To perform the job: When you think that you have done enough, do a little more; one more thing, one more time. Do it in an area that is important to your organization.

**To positively affect others:** Instill confidence and competence in people by setting a good example. Also:

- Clearly communicate that you have his back.
- Give a challenging stretch assignment.
- Empower her to make decisions along agreed-upon guidelines.
- Make him feel safe to take a risk.
- Allow her to fail and then let her discover her mistakes on her own.
- Allow him to complete tasks with minimal micromanagement.
- Compliment; tell her when she did a good job.
- Ask for his recommendation.
- Ask her opinion outside of her area of expertise to show that you think she's an all around intelligent person.
- Appreciate and celebrate his work.
- Reward her in a timely manner with thoughtful gifts like choice assignments.
- Publicly acknowledge his work among peers; then share those accomplishments with leadership; and give him written affirmation.
- Be a good listener.
- Treat her as if she can do the job even if she isn't so sure herself. Give a couple of examples of how she has handled previous tasks and why you think she can do it again.
- Introduce him to others in a complimentary way.
- Believe in her but give her the tools to live up to it.
- Let him fill in for you at a meeting or event.
- Joke around with her.

*"It's my pleasure to work with such a boss. It's nice to be involved and have accountability to prove my abilities."*

If you develop people in this manner, not only will you have stellar coworkers but you will also:

- Gain respect and cooperation
- Get voluntary versus subscriptive followership
- Cause people to achieve what they wouldn't have done without your influence
- Give people the personal power to do great things on their own: dream more, learn more, do more, become more
- Have loyal people who want to remain with you and who will not be attracted to and amenable to answering headhunters' calls
- Be a leader

*"I work at making my people feel valued. They trust me to push them up. They know if they get in trouble, I'll help them, stand up for them, and protect them."*

### MANAGING OTHERS

Do not tolerate poor performance or behavior; address it quickly, firmly, and clearly while still maintaining the person's self-esteem. Do not attack, criticize, or disparage other people's character or motives—that is not for you to judge. You wouldn't want them to judge yours, would you? Then don't do it to them either.

*"It's easy to become a leader. You just say, 'I'll take responsibility for that.'"*

Be neutral, positive, and approving in your approach toward people you deal with. All people. Do not be negative, judgmental, or disapproving in your thoughts because it emotes through your pores, and it shows in your smirks, eye rolls, harrumphs, flaring nostrils, frowns, tone of voice, and choice of words.

Be wholeheartedly neutral if you can't be anything else. Like you, others have a right to have:

- Self-satisfaction
- Self-worth
- Self-regard
- Self-respect

It doesn't get any more basic and real than: Treat them the way you'd like to be treated. As opposed to what I heard the other day: "Do unto others and tell them it was someone else."

What do you do when people provide poor work performance? Address their behavior, but do not attack their *reason, disposition*, or *talent*. Be neutral toward those three areas unless you are proven otherwise.

People need to get approval from you until tested and confirmed that they've made a mistake. Up until the point of proof, it's all-out neutral or positive from you. It's not a gradual thing that you give or take support based on today's behavior. If you withhold sanction until their behavior changes, you are like the mean teacher or the parents who mess up child-rearing. If you find overwhelming evidence that the person is not a solid citizen and you suspect his motive, character, and ability, separate yourself from that person ASAP. This is where you turn the toggle switch off versus on.

As I wrote before, if you have a subordinate whose reason, disposition, or talent is lacking, fire him or her. If you work alongside that person, get away before he or she affects your work. If you have a boss who is that way, transfer or quit.

Talk to people about behavior changes. If you are neutral, positive, or even empathetic toward the person, while still going after a change in behavior, you will have a better chance of succeeding. In other words, you treat the person as adequate; you accept the person for who and what his or she is.

"Joe, you were right with your suggestion about . . . . But when you took charge of . . . , it missed the target. You need to redo this . . . and not do this . . . anymore. Got it?" *ALL* said with a neutral, noncritical, nonjudgmental attitude, a pass-the-salt tone of voice, and a relaxed small smile on your face. If you use a caustic tone of voice and have a frown on your face, you will not instill confidence in the person and you will cause him or her to have less confidence in you.

That is the only way to give correction well. The same words will not be well received if you have a condemnatory mindset.

Give lots of atta-boys—"Uh-huh, sounds good . . . . Thank you . . . . Great work . . . . You're the best . . . . Glad you're on my team . . . "—with voice, video, or written communication. When you note, praise, or appreciate someone, be precise. Instead of "Good job," say, "I liked the way you stood up, looked at the audience, reached for your notes, and started speaking. You really captured them in the first minute."

Do not rescue people. You do not instill confidence if you rescue people. "Here, let me do that for you" can mean "I see you can't do that. You're obviously not smart or talented enough. You need me to save you." Don't correct their work for them; instead work side by side to get it corrected.

Do not become defensive when you are criticized. Don't assume a person is trying to "do it to you." If anything, assume innocence, not arrogance, on the critic's part. Few individuals wake up and think, "How can I harm, hold back, tear down, or at least upset Debra today?" They do wake up and say, "How can I protect me and mine today? If it disrupts or destroys Debra, so be it." That is human nature—survival of the fittest in action.

It's easy to slip into a victim mode and assume someone is trying to *get* you and bully you. Regrettably it's rather easy to be wounded. The rise in power of the downtrodden has never occurred before in the history of the United States—until now. The politics of victimization is the most powerful in this country; the injured party industry is strong and large. In the old days you got your butt kicked if you were a victim. Today you get a financial settlement.

It's distressing when I see a self-decided victim full of resentment feeling his life has been taken from his control and then is given a forum to blame everyone. People need to get the chip off their shoulders. Besides, who hasn't been attacked? Who isn't broken in some way? We all have been wronged at one time or another.

## VIDEOCONFERENCE CALLS

As is true of an audio conference, you are effective (or ineffective) multiplied by the number of people participating. Instead of one viewer's scrutinizing and analyzing you, you have many.

And as is true for an audio conference, you should prepare, be personal, slow down, keep a small smile on your face, use humor, say and take "no," use stories, ask questions, choose optimism over pessimism, pay attention to appearances, and ensure overall that the message you intend is the one you send.

### GOING LIVE

When you go live, swallow your fear. Take a deep breath, or two or three, to relax—it really does work. Expect acceptance. Embrace discomfort. For example, you may not be able to see whom you're talking to even when they can see you. Or there can be time gaps when participants speak: you'll see their lips move but you won't hear the sound until two to three seconds later. And then there are the numerous inevitable unexpected technological glitches you can expect.

Slow down your moving and talking; you want to come across as composed, cool, and collected because you'll make a better impression. Your calm demeanor will also calm and relax others on the call. If you make it easier for them to loosen up and look good in front of others, they will respond more favorably to you.

As you wait for people to join in, put the early video callers at ease with casual questions or comments on national news stories or local ones from the various time zones you're calling into. Don't get into the meat of the conversation until the hard start time.

*"I always get on early and watch when the others come in, grab a cup of coffee, and get set to talk. You can tell a lot about people when they don't realize they're 'live.'"*

At the start time, introduce yourself: "Hello everyone. Debra here. Joining me are Juan, Chelsea, and Blake." When the remote participants introduce themselves, say, "Hello, how are you? Glad you are joining us." Introduce or announce when someone enters the room. In a large group, nominate a chairperson to do the same at his or her location.

*"Get ready to field questions and act or react, whichever is appropriate, in the first 30 seconds. Despite all your preparation, you can walk in and a surprise will pop out at you that you could not have prepared for."*

Speak clearly and a little slower than you might on the phone. Have a calm intensity in your voice, reduce your speed, and keep the pleasant tone despite how agitated you get. Make a point, a compelling sentence, an example, an illustration, or a sound bite that will stick in their heads. Have some statistics or relevant numbers. When speaking, take a moment and pause between points; ask if your point made sense or if anyone has a question.

*"To slow down, I ask a question to take over the room—*
*something the key players are interested in but that's relevant*
*to my experience. I pay attention, and I connect the dots."*

Use voice modulation to get your line of reasoning across; if what you are saying is not very clear, use different ways to express your idea. Don't oversell, mislead, or stretch the truth. Maintain a supersensitive antennae turned to other participants.

Talk, but don't elongate the chatter. Pause enough to think and to avoid nervously blurting out what you say. You can add, "Let me think about that a minute" or "Let me come back to you on that" or "I'll put more thought into it and send an e-mail after the call." When you slow down, even pause, don't do it so long that it encourages someone to jump in if you aren't finished.

As we discussed:

- Engage every *X* amount of minutes to show that you're paying attention. A "Good point" or "Tell me more about that" or a question starting with *who, what, when, where, why,* or *how* would be sufficient.
- Change your body position and angle periodically while keeping your face in the frame. Sitting and looking one way for the whole conversation gets boring to look at even though you are saying brilliant things.
- Periodically check in with a question: "Have I made that point clear? I'll rephrase if you want me to." Do not ask, "Do you get it?" because it makes them look dumb for not understanding you instead of your taking the responsibility of ensuring that you are heard accurately and clearly.
- If a person interrupts you, put one hand up in a stop gesture (again, not right in front of the camera; that's too

aggressive). Then, with an even tone and relaxed smile, continue on. When you finish, ask, "And you wanted to say?"

- When a person is talking, do not cut in, cut off, or interrupt. Even if the person pauses, don't jump in. Wait until you're certain he or she has completed the thought. People hate being cut off or having someone finish their sentences. If you rush or interrupt the person, you're not really listening to what the person has to say, only waiting for a chance to say what you have to say.

- It bears repeating: On video, don't shout, curse, mumble, make distracting sounds with your pen (or other items), nor touch or groom yourself. Don't whisper to others, talk over others, or carry on side conversations.

- Avoid finger-pointing. To avoid figurative finger-pointing, ask questions instead of making statements. To avoid literal finger-pointing, bend the pointer finger in at the first knuckle—now you're knuckle-pointing not finger-pointing. (A gesture adopted by all politicians so as not to look preachy toward the populace.)

---

**ONLINE/OFFLINE: CONTINUOUS LEARNING**

The big advantage of learning is that it enables you to teach others. The best return on investment (ROI) you can get for yourself is from continuously learning. If you don't continue to learn, your ROI will stand for "return on ignorance."

People throw around the expression "Knowledge is power" as if knowledge is to be used to lord over someone. To me, the reason to know more is to be scared less. There are two basic needs in life: procreation and education. The first enables humankind to survive; the second enables you to survive. Ignorance makes simple things 10 times more difficult than they should be and difficult things nearly impossible.

To learn:

- Pick something specific to work on.
- At the beginning, focus on just a small part of it.
- Check yourself to see how you're doing on the minute piece.
- Make note of what you thought was successful and what wasn't.
- Also get opinions from others as to how well you did.
- Make the needed changes the next time.
- Select another small part of the bigger challenge you're working on.
- Repeat the steps above.
- Keep at it a baby step at a time to build, build, build a little more, more, and more.
- Do all the above until it becomes second nature.

Learning agility has to be high on your personal improvement priority list for confidence growth. And you have to exercise it as frequently as you floss. Despite how smart you already are, make it a daily to-do list item to acquire one more piece of useful information every day. (What you learned your friend is doing on Facebook doesn't count.)

The hitch is that most of us, at about the age of eight years old, developed a filter that enables us to take in information that interests us and pertains to us. And it enables us to shut out what doesn't. So we end up dozing off during history if our interests are science or math; tune out English if we're thinking about the Friday night gridiron. If you snuck in catnaps in history or English class in school, remedy that with self-instruction now. It's never too late to discover new interests.

Greedily curious people keep up on everything they can, not just information that pertains to their filtered self-interest. One CEO I interviewed told me he makes it a point to consciously pick something every Monday morning to research that week. He spends the next seven days following where the discovery leads him.

Most CEOs are better informed than the people working for them. *Not* because they are smarter but because they (1) have more people getting them access to extra information, (2) have more people informing them and reporting to them, and (3) have learned to turn themselves into *targets-of* or *owners-of information*.

With the Internet you don't have to depend on your position, academia, a mentor, or school for information and knowledge. It isn't slowly rationed out to you on a need-to-know basis by some outside sources or spoon-fed to you to fit someone's needs. It's all available to you, now.

Shockingly, your bosses don't always support personal edification the way I'm promoting it. Frankly, sometimes, they like you to know just what you know and no more. They might even treat you as if you can walk on water because of your niche knowledge. You become their go-to person. Your selective skill is readily utilized, but you don't get to learn about other areas because people see you, want you, and *need* you in your specialty. Sometimes they support you in getting a second or third degree in your niche knowledge, which frankly can be a step up onto failure's doorstep.

Your specialized field can cause you to become trapped and stuck in that role with less pay and fewer opportunities because they want, and need, you in your area of expertise because they don't have anyone else to do it. To move up, you have to move out into another company.

Recently a national politician, fortunately one term in office before being voted out, spoke on network television: "Information is diversion and distraction." What!?! I couldn't believe my ears. I had to replay it to make sure I heard it right. Being a politician, he wanted you to know the information he wanted you to know, not what you needed to know. Sort of like the manager who wants you to remain in your technical area of expertise and not "dilute your talent" with additional information.

## THE ULTIMATE SELF-LEARNING TOOL

Video is the ultimate self-learning tool. You can video yourself in the privacy of your domain, then play it back. You'll see how you come across and what you should, or could, have done better. You can select one area to improve in, try again, review, and continue to perfection. Then you are prepared to go live in real time with others.

*"If I had a video of me for one day, I'd change. It would be the same as when I catch myself in the mirror and I think, 'Boy, do I look goofy.'"*

When you use the video communication channel or the written communication channel that I will discuss next, you must always remember: Even though you are the only one in your room or space or office at the time, there is someone else on the receiving end of whatever you're doing. Every bit of effort you expend should work to make the other person feel like you are together in the same room or space or office: communicating, resolving, caring, and coming together.

## WHAT'S IRRITATING ABOUT VIDEO?

After polling hundreds of people, here is what they told me irritates them.

When people:

- Don't acknowledge others on the other side of the monitor
- Constantly look bored or continuously check their cell phone

- Don't speak up
- Use cell phones instead of landline phones to call (cell phones usually have poorer connections)
- Join in late
- Don't set up precall arrangements and end up having to spend call time dealing with equipment or call setup issues
- Invite too many people to get on the video
- Have poor backlighting and contrast
- Talk louder than necessary
- Are not aware of their body language
- Don't smile
- Have a background that is too busy or distracting
- On the other end start multitasking
- Talk over others
- Don't mute their phone when appropriate
- Move excessively in and out of view
- Make statements like, "I know you probably can't see this . . . " but then go on to explain a graph or picture without giving details along with the point—that is, "As you see here, the numbers are . . ." versus "This graph shows a 30 percent growth rate"
- Don't pay attention or fidget with laptops and cell phones
- Speak only to the folks in the room, not the people on the other side of the monitor too
- Talk all over each other because of time delay
- Are obviously having private side conversations
- Don't look at the camera or they act stiffly around it
- Shuffle papers noisily
- Do not pay attention to their personal appearance
- Don't operate the data systems correctly
- Eat or drink while on the call
- Use too much hand gesturing

# CHAPTER 3

# *Written Channels*

I n some circles, e-mail is the new snail mail. Nevertheless, universally, it remains a solid communication tool. There is much published on how important a well-written message is for first impressions. Obviously, people can't hear your tone of voice or read your body language so your writing style is going to speak volumes. The impression that you give comes down to who you are and where your mind is, what you have to say, and your consideration of, respect for, and knowledge of the recipient.

Fact
♦ 93 percent of communication comes through voice and body language; only 7 percent through written words. 50 percent of people prefer typing a message over speaking a message.

Before you write your e-mail, stop and think about how you want people to think about you and your missive. Weigh each word carefully. As repeatedly stated, the Golden Online/Offline Rule applies: "Don't send something via e-mail that you wouldn't want to receive yourself." That requires taking time to type, proof, and reproof, and to set up the correspondence for the response you want. One plus side of e-mail is its easy interconnectedness. (Please note that I'm writing about establishing personal connections through e-mail, not e-mail marketing, which is a different type of activity.)

Through e-mail, you can initiate contact with someone

you would feel uncomfortable calling without stuttering and stammering. You can keep up low-maintenance acquaintances with little cost of money or time, and you have the best chance of getting a response because it's easy to click and reply. You can get back in touch with people you've lost track of. And, unlike the phone which is quick and inexpensive too, you can provide a rapid response, while creating a virtual paper trail at the same time. This virtual paper trail "waits for you," as it can be accessed and its information retrieved, even if the e-mail is deleted.

*"You can call 20 times and get no response. Then one e-mail will do the job."*

But as they say, "Anything good taken to the extreme . . . ," and that happens with e-mail too. The ease of use makes for *overuse*. It is also too effortless to include every person and his or her dog into a group e-mail.

*"A company I know limits the use of e-mail and texting to morning only so that in the afternoon work colleagues are forced to get up out of their seat and engage personally with workmates."*

While the easiness of communication is a benefit, the lack of having to actually "look 'em in the eye" gives some people courage to write what they might not have the nerve to say face-to-face. It's easier to hide behind the keyboard when you don't want to deal with an individual directly. It's simple to flippantly throw out careless, hurtful remarks and opinions—even ones that are uncivil and inhuman.

It's sort of like the anonymity driving a car gives you. You slip in behind the wheel, barrel down the road, and brazenly honk your horn or flip someone the bird. These are acts you would never do if you knew the person driving the car next to you or if she could look you in the eyes. Similarly, hiding behind your computer screen, your boldness builds. As you hide from sight, you do not have to talk directly to the person, so you feel that you are not truly accountable.

One female CEO and mother of four had a pleasant routine breakfast with her husband at 7:30 a.m. Monday morning after a weekend of family activities. She left for her work; her husband left for his with a kiss good-bye at 8:00 a.m. At 8:15 he e-mailed her from his car that he would not be coming home as he was in love with someone else.

A magazine editor returned from vacation to find over 3,000 e-mails waiting for her. She sent an auto-response: "I was on vacation and eliminated all e-mails upon return. If yours was important, please resend." She would not likely have said that to someone's face.

*"Don't hide behind the shield of technological anonymity."*

**ONLINE/OFFLINE: SOLVE PROBLEMS—YOURS, THEIRS, AND THE ONES THAT HAVEN'T HAPPENED YET**

The only reason a company hires you is because it has a problem. You have to be a problem solver, and that means a decision maker. In fact, it's a good day for you if every day you open a "new drawer" and there is a problem in it for you to solve. Seemingly unsolvable problems don't disrupt the routine. They are the routine. Everyday vexations are human made, and therefore they can be solved by humans.

It is said you can size up a man or woman by the size of the problems he or she likes to solve. So look for, and go after, big troubles that you can solve or potential problems you can help avoid. Then perform these actions better than others.

*"Relax, and you'll increase your chances of solving your problem."*

Problems are seldom easy; the easy ones have already been solved by someone else. To solve problems:

- Consider the situation from all perspectives involved so you have a rounded outlook on the issue.
- Consider the ideal outcome for all parties involved.
- Look at the problem backward, flip it around and inside out, think of an analogy to some other situation, and talk to someone unrelated to the issue to gain outside perspective on how to solve it.
- Reflect on what you want to avoid.
- Move as swiftly as possible to go after your goal.
- Be flexible and accountable.
- Resolve the problem yourself, and don't bump it upstairs.

As I said, solving requires deciding, so let's talk about decision making.

*"Decisiveness makes a man taller; a woman too."*

### DECISIVENESS IS POWER;
### INDECISIVENESS IS POWERLESSNESS

When you cut through all the junk, life is about choices and decisions in every situation. Very few you make are 100 percent right or wrong. No matter how much you prepare with data, statistics, or other information, you're never completely ready to pull the trigger. As one CEO put it, "It just becomes your turn."

You make choices, and to be happy, you have to make the right choices.

*"I like the feel of my finger on the switch."*

Your inability or unwillingness to make decisions will cause your downfall. *So decide to make a decision and act.* Don't be indecisive; it is unproductive and unattractive to employers, colleagues, and just about everyone else. Worse, if you personally don't decide, someone else will. If you let others make decisions for you, you have to abide by them; and you best not obstruct decisions made by others or lay blame.

I know it's scary because decisiveness means taking responsibility. Nonetheless, to make a decision, follow these steps:

- Identify your objective (a poorly defined goal promotes failure).
- Subdivide the difficult or complicated tasks and information into small chunks that are more manageable.
- Start, continue, and finish with every small chunk; make some decision about each one before going on.
- At a certain point, make an educated, not emotional, guess and decide by yourself.
- Remember, you can always change your mind later.

*"I balance what I know is right with how many people I'll irritate."*

Have information, facts, and figures behind you; be able to make a strong case; be willing to argue your case (even with your boss); and then be fierce about taking decisive action.

*"Don't say, 'I have an idea.' Go make a prototype and bring it to me. That shows decisiveness."*

To help you take the leap, ask yourself, "Will I get sick and die or will a loved one get sick and die from this decision?" If not, go ahead and make it. "Will I lose some security in my sureness?" Yes, but so what? "Will I lose face and lose friends?" Maybe. Who knows?

*"Decision making is a mental colonoscopy."*

I know it can take hours, days, months, and years of hard work to undo bad decisions. However, consider wisely, then pull the trigger and decide. Don't take unnecessarily long amounts of time in making a decision; if you take too long, you might miss opportunities.

Researchers have actually found that people make smarter decisions when they are desperate to use the bathroom. Apparently, a full bladder activates the brain's control circuitry, causing more restraint and savvy decisions—so whatever works. (Honestly, some people choose to study this topic!)

*If you're absolutely sure of your decision,* give your recommendation after getting all of the stakeholders' engagement so they can share in the glory. If you are not sure, take it on yourself to make the recommendation so that others don't share the blame if you're wrong.

Coworkers used to deliberating endlessly over business decisions welcome the efficiency and clarity conferred by decisive leaders. If your organization has a complex network of internal panels and councils for making decisions, change that setup or get out of or out from under that unworkable environment.

If you aren't making at least one decision a day that you are genuinely nervous about, you're probably not trying hard enough.

The day you stop taking risks is the day you stop living.

### E-MAIL BEST PRACTICES

A great way to overcome the lack of a deep connection that often exists in e-mail communication is to establish a relationship, if possible, in person or by phone before using e-mail to communicate. Then, use e-mail when you want to:

- Pass along information
- Have that information documented
- Publicly acknowledge someone's good work
- Reinforce positive behavior and maintain self-esteem
- Give or follow up with a reminder
- Verify understanding of the issues after a complicated discussion
- Support, instruct, and condense
- Sum up quickly
- Reiterate, recap, and clarify
- Introduce people who will be working together
- Set the stage for what's coming
- Reach large groups at a long distance

*"I use e-mails to communicate, appreciate, celebrate, elaborate, and collaborate.*

### THE BETTER THE E-MAILS YOU SEND, THE BETTER YOU GET BACK

Choose your e-mail address wisely. Ihatemyboss2@e-mail.com, for example, may cause people to form a different opinion about you than you want them to. You can have more than one address to use for different purposes, such as business, friends, or online purchases. Fully appreciate that e-mail lasts forever and that anything you write can, and might, be seen by many more people than you intended. You don't want to end up in a situation in which you have to explain, like a politician's spokesperson, "You should have quoted what I meant, not what I wrote."

*"Don't type anything in an e-mail that you wouldn't want everyone to read, because they might, . . . and even if you think it's untraceable, the FBI is very good at finding you."*

Consider whom you are writing to and why. Sometimes e-mails are used to dispense data or solve problems; sometimes to provide therapy and counseling to workers, sooth bruised egos, or resolve conflicts.

Be explicit with yourself as to your goal, which will translate into a better e-mail: "This is what I want . . . , and this is what I don't want from writing this." Be clear in your own mind, or you have little chance of achieving your objectives.

Fact
♦ E-mails are internationally classified as legal and binding documents.

> *"E-mails are guaranteed to take on a life of their own. Count on the fact that parts of yours will be cut and pasted and resent ad nausea."*

Your tone and choice of words, formats, and graphics can be different depending on whom you are sending a message to. A bigger font size for easier reading may work better for some people. More or less formality can be called for with others. And using abbreviations and emoticons to convey meaning may be best with still others.

Symbols, however, can be misinterpreted. (Well, unfortunately everything can be.) One man told me he used a smiley face as a friendly gesture in an e-mail to a new team member in another country. The recipient was quite offended, interpreting the smile as a smirk. Fortunately, the sender sensed a coolness and called to inquire what happened. After a few conversations, the damage was repaired.

Facts
♦ 50 percent of people hate emoticons.
♦ 50 percent love them.

> *"As a rule of thumb, if there is more than one emoticon for every five paragraphs, there are too many."*

Similar to when speaking on the phone, always smile when you type, and imagine that the recipient is in front of you. People sense your attitude. Besides, using an optimistic, good-natured, and gracious tone encourages a prompt response. Consider these two out-of-office replies. Which one was likely written with pleasantness and a gentle smile?

1. Out of office reply. I will be returning to my office on ___. If you need immediate assistance, please contact ___.
2. Hello and thanks for your message! I am currently out of the office. Please contact my awesome business manager Kim at Kimm@xyz.com or my great assistant Connie at Cosgsn@xyz.com for help.

I think option 2 had the small smile.

### WRITE A CLEAR SUBJECT LINE

It may seem simple, but make sure to use meaningful words in the subject line of your e-mail. Make it clear to the recipients why you are contacting them. When writing in the subject line, ask yourself, "Would I open this e-mail based on the title?" Here's an example of a well-written subject line:

Subject: "WHOA . . . your presentation was off-the-charts great!"

Such an e-mail is likely to be read ASAP. The quotation marks also create positive visual differentiation from other e-mail subject lines, making yours a bit more interesting.

Before writing the subject line, consider how you would react to it and answer the question the recipient will most likely ask right off: "What is this, and what does it have to do with me?" Don't be misleading in your subject line.

One executive writes in his subject line how much time it will take the recipient to read the e-mail: "E-mail will take 24 seconds to read." A different tact is to include a deadline; yet another is to include the person's name in the subject line, both of which statistically increases the chances of the e-mail being read. E-mails without a subject more frequently get marked as spam than those that have a subject included.

Sometimes you can say everything you want to in the subject line by giving instructions or supplying a response to a question or concern. If you do reply in the subject line, end it with "#eom" for "end of message," as it will save the recipient from wasting time opening the e-mail, only to find that the total message was contained in the subject line.

Change the subject with each e-mail even if replying. Another good idea is to repeat the subject line in the first line of e-mail. To practice writing enticing subject lines, look at online newspaper headlines—newspaper editors are the masters.

### KEEP IT SHORT AND CONCISE

Your e-mails need to be short, concise, and to the point. Those qualities convey your respect with regard to the recipient's time. You cannot make your message succinct enough. Time is a limited resource for all, so people appreciate when you help them save it. You can safely assume that the person you are e-mailing has already received more than 400 e-mails that day, even before you sent yours.

> "Type the amount of words you could fit on the back of a business card. Don't break the 'long story, short' promise."

Recipients take action more quickly with short e-mails. Long missives are too complicated, ambiguous, and confusing, and they are likely boring. Frankly, it takes more effort to write a short, concise e-mail rather than a long one, but when you put in the effort, you increase the chances of getting your e-mail read and responded to.

*"Figure out your main point. Ask one thing. Edit: find the idea, find the words, find the exact words."*

Use short sentences and two- to three-sentence paragraphs. Avoid long or run-on sentences (stick to 15 words max per sentence). Be short, snappy, and to the point with as much relevant information as possible. Typically try to have no more than three paragraphs in your e-mail, and attempt to say in one paragraph what would take others two. Convey one message per e-mail.

*"To get someone to do five things, send five e-mails."*

Even in brief e-mails, use complete sentences, and use correct spelling, grammar, and punctuation. Write in active, instead of passive, language. Try to write to impress your old high school English teacher. E-mail pithiness doesn't mean you should write like a teenager's text message: "TKS 4 ur time."

*"Today the lines are blurred between the use of proper grammar and being casual, but I think it shows respect to write a real sentence. When people don't, it strikes me as being uneducated."*

Repeatedly test yourself with the question: "How is this useful, helpful, or a benefit to the recipient?" Long e-mails are put aside. If a long, detailed e-mail is deemed necessary, however, differentiate your points and topics by varying the formatting (including the use of bulleted and numbered lists as well as the line spacing); the fonts (including the use of boldface, underlining, and italics); and the colors (*not all of the above in one e-mail*). Make the e-mail easy to read and respond to. Try not to write one so long that you have to put at the end, "In summary."

*"It's amazing what you can tell about a person in a couple of comments based on their punctuation, grammar, and negativity."*

### EXAMINE EVERY WORD YOU WRITE

You appear incompetent when your language is unclear, illogical, verbose, clunky, or full of clutter or clichés. Simplify, prune, and strive for order of thought.

Use easy words. Don't use the same expression over and over and over; use your thesaurus. Instead of, "That was great, . . . we have another great idea, . . . and it would be great if you would . . ." say "That was great, . . . we have another excellent idea, . . . and it would be terrific if you would . . . ."

A one- or two-word sentence can carry tremendous punch as well. Passive words like "Sure" or "That's fine" are borderline rude, blunt, and too direct. Active words like "Perfect" and "Great, go for it," work better.

Use words that project confidence, as opposed to uncertainty. If you use words such as "I know," "I think," "with certainty," "know for sure," "am guaranteed," "am convinced," "undoubtedly," "for sure," "for certain," "definitely," "unquestionably," or "undisputedly," then you are writing with confidence.

> Fact
> ♦ The business leaders of Cowpens, Mississippi, got together and changed the name to Olive Branch, Mississippi. Since the name change, it has become the fastest-growing city in the country.

If you use words like "I feel," "perhaps," "possibly," "conceivably," "seemingly," "likely," "presumably," "maybe," "might," "allegedly," "most," "probably," "could be," "appears," "would seem," or "leads one to think," you don't appear to have much conviction.

Good writing also saves time for the reader. Get quickly to the point. Lead with what's most central, relevant, novel, or important. Your communiqué recipient wants to know quickly, "What's in it for me?"

After writing the e-mail, ask yourself: "What am I trying to say? Have I said it? Is it clear to someone reading it for the first time?" Don't bury your request or purpose (reporters refer to this as "burying the lead"). If the reader has to go to the second screen to find out what you want, the e-mail is ineffective.

To be different and better from most e-mails or letters, start the body of the e-mail with the word "you" instead of "I." "You are the best person to answer this question" or "You were highly recommended by" or "You are in a perfect position to" instead of "I wanted to ask you a question," "I hear you are the person to speak to about," or "I understand you are in a perfect position to . . . ."

A good simple outline:

- The first paragraph is recipient oriented.
- The second paragraph can be you oriented.
- The third paragraph is the wrap-up or next step, and it gives any additional information.

Include the person's name in the body of the e-mail: "Again, Ragesh, you are the best person to give an opinion on . . . ."

*"People love the repetition of their own names."*

In the final draft, see if you can remove the "I's." You will make it oriented to the recipient, not oriented to you, which will increase receptivity. Watch the "me's" too. One recruiter told me if she reads more than five first-person singular pronouns in one e-mail, it automatically goes into the trash.

To minimize back-and-forth, anticipate what the recipient might ask and answer that question first. Think, draft, redo, and then review. Eliminate elements that are not effective. If a sentence is troublesome, get rid of it.

> *"I helped my CEO craft a carefully worded e-mail to his employees. It went through 20 revisions before it was ready to send out. Even if your first draft is really, really good, it's still your first draft."*

Reading your written words out loud causes mistakes to ring in your own ear. You may catch a small or large one and save yourself some embarrassment. Negotiating a contract worth several thousand dollars, a salesperson responded to a request from one of the parties for a time change. The salesperson's response was, "Do hesitate to make that request," which was caught too late and then required the follow-up message: "I meant to write 'do *not* hesitate to make that request.'" Two totally different meanings with the one-word omission. In another instance of a mistake not caught in time, a man took offense when his boss wrote about him in an e-mail, "He's a good buy" when he meant "He's a good guy."

> *"My boss asked me who in her organization could lead a team to solve a difficult problem. I meant to respond with 'Christi,' but I hit Send before the final 'i,' so the answer to her was 'Christ.' My boss replied, 'Oh my, I hope so.'"*

Be careful expressing feelings and opinions versus facts. Try to avoid being negative or responding to negativity. If your message is emotionally charged, walk away from it for some time, and then go back to it, and reread and re-edit the message accordingly.

> *"I wrote an e-mail to my boss about a Public Service Commission initiative, but I forgot the 'l' in 'public.' He called me into his office, and I could tell something was odd, as he was trying to restrain from laughing, when he handed me the printout and asked me to read it."*

Although I'm always for a good-natured or good-humored approach, the reality is that such tactics can be misinterpreted, taken wrong, be offensive to someone, and hurt your message and credibility. Don't let that stop you from trying this approach, but make sure to choose your words carefully.

### USE AN INTERESTING E-MAIL FORMAT

Make your e-mail interesting to look at. Use a line space between changes in the subject or between thoughts the way you would use a pause in a conversation. Add bullet points for easy reading. Or number the paragraphs for differentiating and referencing.

One honcho I know writes his e-mails like this:

To: ____
From: ____

1. To answer your question
on the target date—it's Tuesday.

2. Prior to that, we need to complete
X, Y, and Z.

3. I'm available this weekend to
answer any questions.

4. I'm looking forward to your
recommendations.

All the best, ____

He numbers each brief paragraph, and he inserts a hard return to make 5- to 6-word lines of copy, which, again, are easier to read than a typical sentence like this one, which is 19 words long.

Don't write in caps. Avoid wild and weird colors and fonts. (Some colors are almost unreadable if the e-mail is printed, so stick to black in general.) Refrain from using patterned backgrounds. Don't overuse the High priority, Urgent, or Important options when sending an e-mail. And employing the Read receipt option is generally annoying and intrusive to the recipient.

> *"I received an e-mail written in all caps. My supervisor blamed me and wanted to know what I did to make the person angry."*

Avoid being overzealous with punctuation such as exclamation points. Use hyperlinks, but make sure they work. Don't attach unnecessary files or large files without asking the recipients if that is okay or giving them some type of prior notice.

If you make the e-mail more interesting and easier for the readers, they will understand what you want. You'll also make them feel more efficient in knowing what they are supposed to do, and you'll get done what you need to sooner.

> *"If people will not be getting a chance to meet you in person, then they are going to be basing everything off of your e-mails."*

### BE CAREFUL

E-mail allows you to take action and respond quickly, but you must make sure to do so carefully. Don't forward e-mails or attachments without asking permission or making the recipient aware of the fact. However, also do not naïvely assume that people will give you the same courtesy and respect.

Abstain from forwarding chain letters, jokes, and political rants, especially from your work computer. If someone sends you an e-mail with potentially libelous, sexist, racist, or profane comments in it, do not hit Reply or worse, Reply all. If you are going to respond, originate a new e-mail instead. And don't hit Forward either. Libelous, defamatory, racist, sexist, or obscene remarks in an e-mail have their own legal ramifications. Forwarding (not even originating) such an e-mail is cause for instant job termination in some companies. Keep entrenched in your brain that every communication using corporate media is logged, and you are accountable and potentially liable for everything you write.

Be watchful with your address book, and make sure that e-mails go to the intended people. It's easy to type in the first few letters of someone's address and have a name pop up. Without vigilant reading on your part, however, this address could end up being an incorrect one.

Don't expose your contact's e-mail address by including it in the field; use BCC instead, but make sure BCC doesn't come across as talking behind someone's back. Reply all needs to be reserved for when each and every person on the original e-mail needs to receive a reply—judiciously reserve this function. Some people simply hit Reply all out of laziness rather than writing specifically to people needing a reply. Others use this function to cover their backside when dealing with sensitive information. Some do it just to add those e-mail addresses to their database for future bulk e-mails of their own. All three of these reasons are sloppy and inconsiderate. Such e-mails may not be received favorably, and they will likely cause someone to remove you from their "to include" list.

Don't hit Reply all without *careful* consideration. One person I spoke with in researching this book had this story to share:

Part of my job required seeking employee donations of drug-free urine samples for testing. We sent out a companywide e-mail asking for people's cooperation and promised confidentiality in the results. One—now former—employee hit Reply all rather than Reply with the question: "How long will marijuana use take to pass through my system?"

**ONLINE/OFFLINE: BAD WRITING IS KILLING BUSINESS**

Two of my favorite experts on writing, Howard Zinsser (journalist, nonfiction writer, and author of *On Writing Well*) and Carl Sessions Stepp (senior editor of the *American Journalism Review* and professor of journalism at the Philip Merrill College of Journalism at the University of Maryland), offer these suggestions for smart writing:

- Good words make good sentences, and that makes good e-mails.
- There is no such thing as too much clarity.
- Choose a colorful vocabulary that remains professional so that your messages stick out above the rest.
- Select great words that sparkle, tickle, arouse, stimulate, pump in energy. Don't be bland and mushy.
- Do the unexpected: be jarring, offer a new twist, put drama in.
- Create originality of expression with descriptions, vivid imagery, action words.
- Kill dullness.
- Be simple, not convoluted.
- Use concrete words like "Yikes!" versus "It was a surprise to find."
- Use more periods, fewer commas.
- Keep subjects close to their verbs.
- Use active voice versus passive: "I sent an e-mail to . . ." instead of "the e-mail was sent by me to . . ."

- Cut down on jargon, posturing, buzzwords, and clichés.
- Use a word once, not two or three or more times in an e-mail.
- Slow down and think ahead.
- Use an anecdote, a question, a first-person experience.
- Make it interesting: use fresh metaphors, provide nonsuperfluous details, paint a three-dimensional picture, use a seldom heard quote, scatter in tidbits of unexpected details.
- Share dialogue: "I had dinner with Joe and his boss last night. Nice things were said about you."
- Rethink each sentence, and inspect for legal or ethical problems.
- Cut wordiness.
- Connect but with brevity, humanity, specificity.

Their advice works for e-mails but also for every other manner in which you communicate.

### USE INTERESTING LANGUAGE

Come up with an interesting way of framing what you want to say. Something that makes them stop and think, or smile, or be motivated to respond. Be distinctive. Be accurate. Be in the moment. Don't use catch phrases. Say something personal—not intimate, but something that takes the individual into account. Add some personal element like "Hope you are going to have some fun with your family on the lake this weekend" or "Trust this finds you, Roger, and the children well and happy."

Use a courteous greeting and closing. Vary your salutations. Don't always use the same one. In addition, use them even with a one-sentence e-mail. Speak to the recipient:

Hi Deb. Hope you are well.
Hello everyone, (For group mailings.)
Hey, Deb!
Debra, Hello!
Good Morning, (Or "Afternoon"—be careful with different
time zones.)
Dear friend,
Greetings,

Even though the e-mail time of day and date are included on your inbox, you can add to your greeting, "Tuesday, 8:30 a.m., Good Morning." It's just one more step to make it easier for people.

*"I get annoyed when someone doesn't greet me with a 'hello' or 'good morning.'"*

A young man wrote to me about one of my books and began the e-mail with, "*Gracious, Shukriya, Dhanewaad, Grazie, Schönen Dank, Doh je, Mamnoon, Shukran Gazilan, Sagolun, Ngiyabonga.* Thank you in 10 different languages." That greeting was memorable.

Sign off with a complimentary closing, such as:

My best to you
Sincerely
Cheers
Happy spring (summer, fall, winter)
See you next week (tomorrow)
All the best
Thank you, again
Best to you
Sincerely

Quite sincerely
Take it easy
Be good, do well
Have a great day!

One CEO I interviewed has his e-mail sign off with "Have a nice day" written in 10 different languages.

### USE A BRIEF SIGNATURE

In your signature block, avoid multiple phone numbers and e-mail contacts; pick the one you prefer. If you want the recipients to contact you through an IM program or Skype, you can include that information, but don't add your home, work, or cell phone numbers or your fax numbers unless you really do want people to contact you in those ways. Note, however, that adding your social networking feeds lets people learn more information about your professional activities. Again, include it or not depending on whom you're writing to. You can have different signature versions for different types of e-mails: to a client or customer; to your boss; to your friends; and to your colleagues.

*"You don't need a signature block to be longer than your e-mail."*

Reconsider including quotes since they, like humor, can be misinterpreted. Moreover, including quotes can break the "be brief" rule. Unless required to do so in your company, avoid the legal disclaimer add-on. If you're responding to e-mails from a device that doesn't have a spell-checking feature in the software, a sign-off with "Sent from my Windows mobile; please excuse any typos or unintended brevity" covers spelling or wording errors.

If you include a photograph of yourself, make sure it has a high enough resolution and pixel count for the best quality. Also, use a photograph in which you look awake, alive, and alert. A photo or sketch gives people someone to "see," to relate to, and to focus on when they are online. This is the time for the big smile: the "glad to meet you and happy to be here" one. A small smile isn't enough. A driver's license mug shot isn't the way to go either.

It was pointed out to me by a young entrepreneur that nearly all of the venture capitalists he deals with online use photographs of themselves, but the photographs are in half-frame where only half of the face is in the photo. Perhaps it's edgy and trendy, but it also looks half-upfront. CEOs of public companies could never afford to use half-frame photographs of themselves because it would imply that they were hiding something.

It's always a good idea to study what the "best" do and then pick from that. Peruse online or offline publications for avatars that speak to you. But as you age, have your age-appropriate photograph updated. It's ridiculous when I'm on the program with a fellow speaker who has an airbrushed vanity photograph in the program, and then I meet the person and wonder why he sent his parent instead.

### ANSWER AND REACT PROMPTLY

When responding to an e-mail, answer as promptly as possible. You create stress on yourself and others when you don't answer. Unofficial etiquette is to reply between 20 minutes and 2 hours. Attempt to acknowledge your receipt of others' e-mails within 24 hours. You don't have to act on them, but do reply with "I will get back to you later" at least. That said, if you can act on an e-mail too within that time frame, that would be efficient— just as you try to handle a piece of mail literally once by doing something with it when you open and read it, try reading an e-mail once and then, similarly, something with it right then.

*"E-mail stress is caused when messages pile up. It's an all too physical manifestation of the myriad of responsibilities weighing you down."*

Do answer back even if the sender does not expressly request it. Assume he or she expects one. Ask for a response if you want one; don't assume the recipient knows you are waiting for one.

Reply to all questions: it's irritating to senders when you skip one or more and they have to re-send the same request.

Sometimes there is a lot of back-and-forth, and just as if this occurred when you were talking to someone in person, you wouldn't stop suddenly, the same holds true with e-mails. You need to continue the conversation until it is completed. It's a good practice beyond four to five back-and-forth exchanges to stop e-mailing and call instead. Save long exchanges for the phone; they will become too cumbersome in e-mails.

Follow through with whatever you commit to doing. It's dishonest to say you'll respond later or perform some duty in the e-mail but then don't do so.

When you send an e-mail, you are creating obligation for the recipient. Upon seeing the e-mail, the recipient has to spend the next 20 seconds deciding if and what to do to handle it: "If I have this, I'm supposed to do something with it."

Hold out no expectations. You really aren't owed a response just because you wrote an e-mail. It's standard social courtesy to reply, yes, but there is no law requiring a response.

So make it clear, easy, and desirable to answer your e-mail. Respond readily to others' initiatives as a matter of practice, regardless of their habits. Everything you do gets noticed by someone—positive or not so. I was told of a CEO who sent e-mails to his people at 6 a.m. on Christmas morning—and they weren't about Santa Claus! The recipients felt stressed to act in response or risk looking as though they were unfocused on the year-end deadline.

A female recruiter sleeps with her BlackBerry. When I asked, "Doesn't it bother your husband for you to get calls in the middle of the night?" She responded, "I don't care. I need to be accessible." (I'm thinking that the marriage isn't going to run too smoothly!)

Even if others are inconsiderate with demands on you, don't reciprocate. To prevent feeling obligated unnecessarily, set limits beforehand as to when and how you can be reached and stick to it. Don't be rigid, of course; if common sense says respond, do. But in most cases, it will be perfectly acceptable to the sender to hear back from you within your normal working hours.

---

**ONLINE/OFFLINE: MISTAKES YOU'LL MAKE AND WHAT TO DO ABOUT THEM**

In an attempt to avoid mistakes, many people think it's best to say nothing, do nothing, and be nothing. Not taking action, however, will turn out to be your biggest mistake!

*"I suggest you try to make mistakes one at a time with a lot of time in between."*

Blunders come in many forms. You:

- Assumed things were the same today as they were yesterday or even after lunch
- Were afraid to pick up the phone and call someone who's intimidating
- Failed to consider the future significance of what you said or did
- Said something behind someone's back and not to his face
- Expected someone to keep a secret
- Didn't follow your instincts or intuition

- Assumed others operate under the same rules that you do
- Didn't keep every promise made (or every promise people thought you made)

No matter how smart you are, you can still get snookered. Sometimes mistakes are made when you put your trust in someone who turns out to be conniving in some way or flat out lying. You might get lazy, full of hubris, or just a little stupid, causing your decisions to fizzle, backfire, bomb, or explode. Overconfidence or a lack of due diligence can create a world of problems. If you make a mistake, however, admit it right away. A cover-up is worse than the original transgression—if you don't take responsibility, it shows you are deceitful too.

When you make an error, don't allow the moment to swallow you whole, and don't let it turn into a public skewing either. Calm and slow yourself down. Say, "My apologies." Do something to fix it and make up for it. (And don't reach for a Manhattan, scotch, or cheap wine; you can drink a smoothie if it helps though.)

*"Every time I mess up, I put a new song on my iPod."*

Think of playing a video game: Most of the time when you're playing, you're losing. You don't beat yourself up about making mistakes. The same should be true in real life: If you try something that doesn't work out, go back and try again. That's how the game works, and as it turns out, the most fun parts of a game are when you're losing.

*"I like the thrill of the possibility about making a mistake."*

You aren't judged by your successes as much as how you handle your missteps. Even if you are the boss, it's okay to be wrong. In fact, it's good to be wrong and for your subordinates to be right.

Such situations show you are helping them grow, and when they grow, it takes a load off your back from doing all the heavy lifting!

*"I was in charge. I'm really very sorry about the pain and suffering and loss that resulted. I take full and complete responsibility."*

When you need to make an apology for something:

- Take action sooner rather than later
- Don't avoid and skirt the issue (the way politicians do when they routinely refer to their mistakes as "oversights")
- Think through what you want to say
- Phrase it carefully, write it down, and rehearse it
- Plan where, when, and how you'll say it
- Be genuine and sincere when you express regret
- Take responsibility. Don't try to justify, find a scapegoat, or shift culpability. Explain the actions to be taken going forward to prevent a repeated incident. Explain the change that you will make to remedy the wrong: "Here's what I'm doing. . ."
- Make amends and reparations, and make the situation right
- Explain the likely penalty if you don't carry out your commitment

Then, truly live the way you promised, as that's the only thing that will rebuild trust.

Your candor might win public sympathy and support since showing humility plays to people's taste for tales of failure and redemption (sort of like scrappy underdogs). Remember though, an apology must be a sincere act of contrition, not an act of containment. Be grateful that time heals. True, the bigger the transgression, the longer the time to heal. But in time, people will forget if you stick with the change you say you'll make.

*"It's a huge confidence builder to realize that you can fix almost anything and that there is no crisis that you cannot manage. I have very little fear of failure. I know what it looks like, and I know I can rebuild."*

Make your share of mistakes. Setbacks make you a little harder and make you work smarter. Go forward and maybe fail. Turn away and definitely fail.

Every honest CEO will tell you that he or she fails more often than he or she succeeds. You never eliminate missteps, but you can grow to minimize their size and impact.

### WHEN NOT TO USE E-MAIL

Never, ever give bad news first with e-mail. Have the courage to tell the person in person or at least on the phone (not via voice mail) at the outset. After you have spoken with the person, you can confirm, add on, or follow up with an e-mail.

Don't e-mail but phone or get up and go see the person when you:

- Assign blame
- Have a sensitive topic with thin-skinned people involved
- Give criticism or negatively evaluate performance
- Need to communicate anything that attacks overtly or covertly
- Say "no"
- Apologize
- Have a huge amount of information that you need to thrash out
- Need to say something that could be easily misinterpreted

Send all potentially sensitive e-mails to the Draft folder before sending them out, and then reread them later before you actually send them. Better yet, put your own address into the To: box so if you accidentally click Send, it goes to you. Fill in the correct To: after you've written and repeatedly proofed the content of the e-mail.

Fact
♦ 80 percent of e-mails require additional clarification.

*"Write your e-mail, reread your e-mail, reread your e-mail, and reread your e-mail."*

If you are the recipient of an e-mail that makes you mad or irritates you, do not phone or write back immediately. Rushing in the digital age can severely damage a relationship. Take some time to free yourself from the irritation. Clear your head of any knee-jerk reactions. Sit down, close your eyes, put your head back, and visualize your preferred outcome.

Slow everything down. Do some transcendental meditation; find a Zen-like calm. Say a prayer if that's your style. Play solitaire or computer chess. Listen to some music. Never ever rush to respond to an irksome e-mail.

*"Before I answer, I always go on a five-minute walk."*

Refrain from profanity. True, it's frequently heard in rap music, primetime television, and over White House microphones. Yes, it lets you ventilate, and studies show it relieves the pain you're in. Still, it can distance you, cause a breech, and a little "I'm okay, you're not" feeling.

Instead of snapping back with:

- That makes no sense.
- Are you stupid?
- Are you crazy?
- Are you an idiot?

- Why are you being so difficult?
- Don't you get it?

ask:

- What are you really asking?
- What are you really saying?
- What is your purpose or motivation for this approach?
- What do you need from me to clarify or correct the situation?

When you've emotionally settled down, draft an appropriate response. Read it out loud to see how it sounds to you. Send it to yourself, and examine it as if you were the recipient of it from someone else. Have a coworker read it, and get his or her take on the tone and likely reaction. Write to solve a problem, not create one.

If an immediate response is required but you are not ready to send one due to your emotional reaction, let the person know you are constructing a response. Do not let the sender's demand for a response make you stressed or uptight and then rush to respond. Instead, respond when you are able to write what you need to in the best manner possible.

Recognize the fact that no matter how much time and effort you put in to make it the perfect missive, you never know how someone will take it. One CEO told me about his crafting a complimentary note to one of his people. He clicked Send, and within 30 seconds he received an e-mail back from the recipient, "What the hell do you think you're doing? Why did you write a note like that?" The recipient had misinterpreted the praise and somehow took it as intense criticism. "We finally got it understood, and he accepted my intent. When we ended the misunderstanding, I kidded him with, 'You can bet that I'm never going to send you a note of appreciation again,' but in hindsight it's likely he misunderstood my humor then too!"

## TEXT MESSAGES

Text messages are an expedient substitute for e-mails. Texting is ideal for times when it is impossible, inconvenient, undesirable, impractical, or unacceptable to make voice calls. It's also great for alerts, news, reminders, updates, and confirmations.

While texting is a fast bidirectional way to communicate, it also gives you the chance to think of what you want to say. If you are with someone in person or on the phone with someone and you take a long time to respond to his or her questions, it's a little strained. In contrast, a delay in responding to a text message is accepted. When you have some time to think, you respond better.

**Fact**
♦ 31 percent of people polled prefer to be reached via a text message over any other medium.

All the suggestions for e-mail apply to text messaging as well:

- Apply the Golden Online/Offline Rule "Text unto others as you'd have them text unto you."
- Be briefer than brief.
- Solve problems; don't create them.
- Consider who your recipient is.
- Smile when you type.
- Have what you say be useful, worthwhile, interesting, and helpful.
- Examine every word.
- Use correct spelling and grammar.
- Don't attack, criticize, or assign blame.
- Don't text when you're angry or mad or when you've been drinking.

A good use of text messages is to write to someone you want to talk to and ask if he is available to talk. To many people, phoning directly is considered intrusive, inappropriate, unproductive, and discourteous—sort of like walking into an office unannounced and expecting to talk to the person. Texting is also useful when:

- You need something quickly, and an e-mail is likely to get overlooked in an inbox.
- You need to dispense small amounts of data to one individual or a group.
- You are in a situation in which you can't phone or talk to the person.
- You don't want to wait for the person's usual e-mail checking time.
- You don't want to talk to the person directly.

Fact
▶ In tests, texting while driving has been shown to have a bigger negative impact on driver safety than being drunk.

*"I text when I think someone may pick up the phone and I don't want to make the small talk about the weather or whatever but just want to give them some quick information."*

The time not to text is when an in-person meeting or phone call is faster and more personal, or when a resolution can be achieved more effectively in person—oh, and while you are driving!

### TEXT MESSAGE BEST PRACTICES

Limit texting when you are face-to-face with another person. Keep your thumbs still while talking to someone. If your electronic messages are more interesting and important than the people you are with, you need to change your attitude (or the people you're with). Do not text in front of subordinates because it shows no respect to them and it may make them feel humiliated and demeaned, like a child with adult parents talking about adult things.

Texting is so easy to perform that it can be done anywhere and in almost any circumstances. But the problem with texting everywhere is that you give continuous partial attention to everything else going on around you. You see people hunched over, hands under the table, staring at their crotch in a staff meeting, on a conference call, in the library, in church, in the classroom, and almost anywhere, and everywhere, else.

> *"There are skilled people who can look you in the eye but have their hands in their pocket texting."*

One young man explained that he felt it was only honest to text openly in a meeting instead of sitting there acting as if he was listening. If you overuse that approach—constantly updating your cyber interactions in front of other people and relying only on new technologies to communicate—some people, especially those who may not prefer texting over other forms of communication, will be turned off and not want to interact with you in person. They may truly become virtual as they walk away from you, your input, and your work! (Anything good taken to an extreme can become negative.) That's when one texting shortcut is especially fitting: step away from the keyboard (SAFTKB).

> *"Am I rude to look at my cell phone when I'm in a meeting with you? Well, I consider it rude when I'm playing a video game or reading a book online and someone wants to talk to me. I'm busy, and if I wanted to interact with you, I wouldn't be playing a computer game or reading."*

Do not, however, get irritated when others text while in your company. If it's your team members doing it, lay out ground rules in advance: "We'll take a break for texting every five minutes before the half hour. Please pocket your phone until then." Without exception, set the example with your own exemplary behavior. With a good-natured attitude, send a text that says, "I'm right in front of you. Please put down the phone," if people forget.

With text messages, you can shorten words with abbreviations and pictogram symbols, but you shouldn't do so. I know on a phone it's a small keyboard and thus difficult to type at length. I appreciate that it's commonly accepted to abbreviate—even cool and "with-it" looking. I realize it's faster. I also know there are lots of times people end up having to phone you and ask "What did you mean?" because they received overly cryptic messages.

*"I had a young, new hire who couldn't write anything over three letters in length. He wasn't dumb, but it made him look dumb."*

In a professional or formal setting, the use of texting language can make a bad impression.

It's conceivable that in a few years the English language will morph into something that is more efficient and includes standard texting abbreviations as young people get into the workforce using this communication channel. But until then, set yourself apart by using complete, but pithy, sentences instead of abbreviations.

Lastly, steer clear of "sexting" (sending explicit or suggestive messages) at the office. Whether you are a CEO, a member of Congress, or a teenager, you'll likely regret it.

### WHAT'S IRRITATING ABOUT E-MAIL?
After polling hundreds of people, here is what they told me irritates them.

When people:

- Give no greeting or sign-off
- Provide incomplete information
- Send messages that have typos and poor punctuation and sentence structures
- Put quotes or sayings in their signatures
- Expect a reply in five minutes
- Ask questions that can't be answered in an e-mail and that require a phone call
- Sound cold or inhuman
- Write overly short, curt messages
- Send long e-mails or send long e-mail chains that I have to go back into to get context while they write, "What do you think?"
- Don't reread their words to determine if the wrong unwritten message was sent
- Send e-mails with mixed topics
- Use subject lines that don't reflect the e-mail's content
- Repeatedly put in the subject line "Please read" or "Urgent"
- Don't use the addressee's name
- Forward e-mails without asking
- Don't respond
- Send something important via e-mail that deserves a phone call instead
- Send an e-mail rather than having the courage to talk to me directly
- Type with bold, caps, wild fonts, or red text
- Sit close by but send an e-mail instead of getting up and stopping by my office to ask a question
- Give one-word answers to complicated e-mails

- Don't bother to read the e-mail trail and respond blindly
- Send long e-mails without paragraphing
- Don't include a phone number or any other optional contact information
- Lazily hit Reply all when individual, targeted responses are necessary
- Write in an emotional state
- Take a tone in written form they'd never take in person
- Write as if they were in an informal conversation instead of being engaged in business correspondence
- Use abbreviations and emoticons

### WHAT'S IRRITATING ABOUT TEXT MESSAGES?

After polling hundreds of people, here is what they told me irritates them.

When people:

- Text back-and-forth when a simple conversation in person or on the phone would be more efficient
- Utilize too many abbreviations or they use slang or nonwords
- Write back so quickly that I feel obligated to write back to them quickly; when they exaggerate the urgency
- Assume my phone plan accepts the messages
- Don't respond
- Send unimportant messages
- Do noncritical texting during a meeting or when with someone
- Drive and text
- Send information that I need to retain
- Overuse it and will communicate only this way
- Send long messages that should be put into e-mails

- Assume I am available to respond 24/7 (they are obsessed with connectivity)
- Use bad grammar
- Read and respond to texts while I am talking to them
- Leave the notification sound on in public places
- Send text messages that are so long that it takes two or three separate messages

# CHAPTER 4

# Online Communities Channels

Boomers schmooze, generation Xers network, and generation Y goes on social sites. But their purposes are the same: to connect, meet up, develop affinity, bond, share, and learn. Regardless of whatever route you choose, it's about building relationships grounded in friendships. Today's online community will help you do all that—it's like networking on steroids!

**Facts**
♦ If Facebook were a country, it would be the third largest behind China and India.
♦ 1 out of 12 people are on Facebook, and 66 percent of those people come back to the site every day.
♦ For every 6 minutes you're on the Internet, 1 minute is on social media sites.

*"I gave up Facebook for Lent. That was a bigger sacrifice than chocolate ever was."*

Despite the inviting proliferation of the social media landscape, to be competitive now, your connecting endeavors require a two-prong approach:

1. Put the laptop down. Jump into your car or catch the subway, go across town, physically walk into a room of people, grab a drink, grab a hand, shake, talk to someone, then go talk to someone else, then someone else. Jump back into your car or onto the train, go back across town, and return home both exhausted and energized by whom you met and what you learned.

2. Log on to your favorite online social media or community site and constructively participate.

It could seem like the second option is greener, cheaper, and easier, so you can therefore rationalize relying on that single approach. Wrong. Social media networking is not a substitute for in-person contact but rather an addition to it; both are compulsory. Online networking is just a step, not an end goal. Of course, social media involvement is an important step in the virtual workplace. If you don't keep up with the latest in this communication channel, you'll be even further behind when the next new thing arrives. (If you aren't using social media, people will wonder what's wrong with you.)

Whether online or offline, the extent to which you benefit from social media depends on your activity. If you are reluctant to participate in online networking, you will sabotage your own career before any business bully ever has a chance to.

A flawed use of any networking endeavor is to prove your importance to the world. Social media networking is not there for you to engage in digital narcissism: posting for attention to make sure people think about you and your every interaction.

A flawless use is to learn what others know and to share with them what you know. Whether through online networking or in-person conversation, simultaneously sharing what you both know creates a give-and-take, mutually beneficial relationship.

### APPOINT YOURSELF YOUR OWN CHIEF SOCIAL MEDIA OFFICER

When you are networking in person, you present a certain image that you want people to take away. It might be that of a seasoned leader, a sophisticate, an eccentric, a trust fund baby, a geek, a financial whiz, or simply a person who is memorable, impressive, credible, genuine, trusted, liked, cool, calm, collected, competent, confident, and comfortable. Online you must develop and craft your reputation of choice too. If you don't, some algorithm will do it for you.

That's why you are your own chief social media officer: to create your own image and shape the perception people make of you, monitor the way you are seen, and correct misinformation and defend your reputation when necessary. Think about your objective and your goal. Prepare compelling content (in your profile and your posts) that supports that objective and goal.

Listen to conversations. See what issues are bubbling to the top as you monitor Q&A boards, answer and ask questions, read industry blogs, survey friends and fans, then cultivate connections.

The social media communication channel, ahead of all others, lets you initiate seeking out people who inspire you and whom you admire; those you want to learn from and choose to emulate. These people are often also the ones you can reach only through the Internet that you'd normally not have access to.

To connect with these people, first, read what these people have written themselves as well as what has been written about them; watch their speeches, interviews, and webcasts; study their profile; and find out their likes and dislikes. Second, learn what interests them. Third, look for connections where you can be helpful to them in getting what they want. If you do that, you'll end up getting what you want too.

**ONLINE/OFFLINE: BE UNDAUNTED**

Online and offline, people follow others who are confident: the undaunted.

When you are confident (not counterfeit), you:

- Are more fun to be around
- Attract people who are like-minded
- Don't get jealous of others

- Have courage
- Are decisive
- Don't fear mistakes
- Aren't easily embarrassed
- Won't freak out
- Accept the inevitably of moments of self-doubt
- Perspire but take action anyway

People accept your opinion of yourself. If you have a low opinion, people take it; if you have a high opinion, they take that too, at least until they have a reason not to. It's their starting place in how they perceive you. So play the part of the undaunted.

*"I had many years of having to bluff my way through. I just danced around with confidence. Down deep I was churning with anxiety."*

Few new CEOs, managers, or bosses think in their heart that they are qualified for the job when they get it. They aren't going to tell you that though! But it's true. Everyone you meet has a level of insecurity and inadequacy; the variance is in his or her ability to camouflage these worries.

*"I do what every other CEO does: go into a dark room, bend over, vomit, straighten myself up, and go back out there."*

It's arrogance, not confidence, when you:

- Assume you know it all
- Think you're smarter than others
- Don't listen and learn
- Are full of bluster; too sure of yourself in every situation without reason
- Abuse your power, or browbeat, demean, or put down other people

- Act superior
- Think "I'm special. The rules don't apply to me."

*"If you go to work to reward your ego, you'll have a tough time."*

To build undauntedness, swallow your fears, and every day do something that scares you. Step away from your self-focus and out of your comfort zone, and do something different than you'd normally do.

An audience member came up to me after a seminar eager to tell me this story. She was the lowest-level newbie at a behemoth company, and almost as a joke, she was given the task to wear the company mascot outfit at an executive offsite meeting with the corporate board of director members. She was in total disguise in her padded body suit and oversized head piece, and she was carrying a rubber billy club, which were all part of the outfit. Standing beside the CEO as he addressed the crowd, she took her stick and poked him in the belly. He laughed good-naturedly (as did everyone else), and he reached over and put his arm around her in a mock wrestling hold, tousled her hair on top of the headpiece. She said, "So I did it again. I felt so powerful, but I'm ashamed it took the costume to hide behind to make me feel confident around him."

Now I'm not recommending you poke your boss in the belly with a billy club. I am just saying that there is room for trying new things.

**OVERALL, DO THE OPPOSITE OF WHAT PEOPLE EXPECT: GO AGAINST THE GRAIN**

Several times in this book I've mentioned one thing you consistently must do to become more memorable, impressive, credible, genuine, trusted, liked, cool, calm, collected, competent, comfortable, and confident. This one thing will help bring out these qualities in others as well. When you boil it down, this one thing is intelligently observing what most people do and then not do the same thing. Do the opposite (without being weird, of course). Use your common sense, but don't be common in your actions.

Listen to your initial instinct, and then do the reverse. I'm not saying be obstinate or be contrarian just to be contradictory. What I am saying is be sure to examine the alternative actions open to you. It keeps people on their toes around you, makes life more fun, and will likely improve the situation you're in. (I can guarantee that doing the same things over and over again won't lead to any positive advancements.)

Doing the reverse of what is expected is particularly effective with the most resistant person in the room. Consider taking the following actions:

- Ditch your routine. Do the don'ts. Do them when it doesn't matter so you are practiced when it does. If you've been sitting, stand. If you've been standing, sit. If you've been traveling, stay home. If you've been staying home, get out and travel. If you've been teaching, go learn something new. If you've been learning, go teach something. If you've been talking, be quiet and listen. If you've been listening, speak up and talk.
- If people with the "right" skills fail to solve the problem at hand, assign people with the "wrong" skills to solve it.
- If you have bad news, instead of avoiding telling people because you are nervous about their reaction, disarm them by being the first to bring it up and before they hear it elsewhere.
- When times are superserious, bring in a little silly. When something is silly, bring in the serious to get back on track.
- When you get a new boss, start your work with the new boss as if the person with the new job is *you*.

Seek the opposite in everything. One medical journal reported findings that people slip and fall less on wintry icy footpaths if they wear socks on the outside of their shoes. (Maybe not the first impression you want to make when you walk into the office, but you get the idea.)

Then again, there are some things you shouldn't do the opposite of. For example, if your company is committed to excellence, don't be committed to incompetence. If it's common courtesy to be polite on the phone, don't choose that one to do the opposite. Use your brain in employing the "opposite" method.

### INVEST YOUR TIME

Take at least four minutes a day. Why four? Regardless of how busy you are, you can carve out four minutes for some online connecting activity. Just 1 of the following suggestions implemented every day gives you 360 interactions in a year (giving you a few days off for holidays):

- Introduce two people who'd like to meet.
- Suggest sites of interest.
- Forward articles or links.
- Tag good information you're seeing.
- Send an invitation.
- Give a recommendation.
- Share your experiences in a blog.
- Pose questions to see the advice that peers and experts give.
- Answer questions.

The return on your investment of time is becoming known and being remembered and sought out for your expertise. Obviously, don't get weird about your online involvement; do not stalk, obsess, persist, and pester. Just put what you think might be of interest out there and leave it alone.

In this chapter, I'm not focusing on any specific social feed—

you likely have found your favorite communities whether you are a late arriver or early adopter. Moreover, the intricacies of how to maximize the usability of various feeds changes too rapidly for book publishing. What is hot now will cool and be replaced by something hipper, more specialized, less cluttered, and easier before you finish reading this chapter. Note that I'm also writing about your personal use of social feeds as opposed to corporate marketing and promotion use.

### REMEMBER YOUR VULNERABILITY IN YOUR SOCIAL NETWORKING

As is true of all of our associations with others, there is potential vulnerability in communicating via the Internet. E-mails (and voice mails) are not private; disclaimers to such are nearly useless. You never know who is going to receive a forwarded e-mail, listen to your voice mail messages, or read your texts. The lack of privacy in social media is about 1,000 times more true.

Your online content is tattooed on the Internet, and it is not even a tattoo in a private place. Privacy is a thing of the past; there are few hiding places. As they say, "What happens in Vegas stays on Facebook."

*"Don't think for a second anything you post is private."*

Lawyers find digital discovery; police solve crimes; your boss can (and likely does) check in on you via Twitter or Facebook; and 80 percent of companies recruit from social networking sites.

Each word you write is indexed by these sites and stored under your name (or your alias). Real-time searches and search engines will produce your latest comments as soon as someone types in your name—every detail is traced back to you. People can access information even if they aren't your friends or followers.

*"We are a data mining company, and we watch people who don't know they are being watched."*

Everything gets recycled and republished—especially things you shouldn't say. People find this information the most interesting: anything to do with sex, politics, money, or religion generally fall into that category.

*"As an openly gay manager, I look on Facebook to see if a job candidate is a fundamental Christian."*

Aside from the innate transparency of online communities, there is the law: the Freedom of Information Act requires access to information you put out there.

*"Digital dirt is worse than a tattoo, and it follows you forever. You don't get fired from what's on there because you won't get hired. No one will call you for an interview."*

Don't inundate social networking sites with useless information, and don't overshare all things big and small. Overexposure can be potentially harmful to your reputation and flat out embarrassing. Guard what remains of your privacy.

Fact
⬧ 100 million photos are put on social networking sites per day.

*"In defense of all the photos posted: with young people putting everything online, the standards of behavior will be relaxed, and since everyone has done something he or she is not proud of in his or her lifetime, these indiscretions will eventually appear only human."*

You can give enough information to let people know you and still maintain some discretion. Oversharing is far worse than undersharing.

## YOUR ONLINE REPUTATION EXISTS WHETHER
## YOU DO ANYTHING ABOUT IT OR NOT

Unless you are so far off the grid that you live in an abandoned vehicle on blocks, the IRS does not know you exist, your siblings assume you are dead, and your fingerprints have been surgically removed, there are some electronic records on you. (Of course, if any of the above is true, you probably aren't reading this book.)

Facts
♦ 66 percent of CEOs have no involvement in social media because they perceive there to be a risk that sensitive information will be divulged and because they don't want to make the time commitment.
♦ 33 percent of CEOs use social media for highly controlled communicating such as posting a letter on the company website.

If someone runs a Google search on you, something is likely to come up. The good stuff are articles, stories, and blogs that you've written or been quoted in; awards, announcements, projects you've been part of; and profiles, postings, tags, and "likes" on social feeds. Then there are the things you have little control over that come from public records and what others post.

*"Only the very, very rich or powerful can remain un-Googleable."*

It is common that if you contact someone out of the blue, before she considers responding to you, she will run a Google search on you and check your Facebook and Twitter posts.

### THINK TWICE BEFORE YOU POST

When you engage: think twice, post once. Be interesting so you're appealing to get to know. How you express yourself, how you think, and how you handle and present yourself all add up to the impact you have.

Understand the culture of the media site that you are using, and communicate only about topics appropriate for the site. It's okay to lurk a little in a new community you've joined to get a feel for it before posting messages. You'd do the same at a live event; step back and observe before joining in.

Ask yourself, if your post is:

- Relevent
- Engaging
- Positive and pleasant
- Accurate and honest
- Valuable
- Edgy
- Controversial
- A hot topic

Does it:

- Stimulate conversation?
- Give insider information?
- Provide little-known data?
- Teach something?
- Prompt other sites to link?

*"When you post, 'wow' people with content: solutions, tips, advice. Be worth talking about."*

Don't post silliness just to add another item. Share stuff that has a reason for showing. Avoid random quotes, statements, useless updates, rants, and repetition. Watch for typos and grammatical errors in your posts just the way you do when you use written and voice channels. Exhaustively edit everything you post. Use impulse control. There is no machine to take you back in time and unpost. The Internet is a permanent record;

it never forgets anything published. Comments, news, images, blog posts, commentary, status updates, or photos placed on the Internet dissipate like airborne viruses.

Slow down. Even though you can post or respond with a few keystrokes and a click, don't. Sit on it, walk on it, sleep on it. Then reword it.

> *"Do the firefighters' drill: stop, drop, roll. Stop the process. Drop the idea that you're emotionally wedded to. Roll into a better way of wording."*

Filter what you write. Ask yourself if it is what you want your boss, coworkers, parents, children, and grandparents to read—because they will, or someone will tell them about it.

> *"One site profile was more detailed in its questions than a psychological profile I had to complete to go to sniper school."*

People can be in such a hurry to get their message out into the media stream that they don't think seriously about the repercussions until it's too late. It's not just the information you dispatch. Someone else can take a photo of you and tag you, and it is there without end too—your personal Wikileaks moment. And before you post about others, put yourself in their position to make sure it won't offend them.

> *"I run a public company. You don't have to dig too deep to get some dirt on me."*

A good question to repeatedly ask yourself as you pause to post is, "Ten years down the road when I am chief *something*, do I want that out there?"

Don't let the fear of the openness be an excuse not to engage. Use your common sense as to what you want to share and stop there. Strongly remember that a protected message, a direct message, and a secure connection do *not* always work. At the least, hiccups happen and technology fails. (There are some members of Congress who have learned this the hard way.)

*"Never post to a social site when drinking."*

To be more secure in your posting:

- Check your privacy settings (but don't trust them).
- Choose your privacy settings such that you will not be visible to your entire list of friends; separate your list of friends into work, family, best friends, and so on.
- Check out (log off) of websites when you're finished.
- Change passwords frequently.
- Set whom you allow to see your "likes"; many of the buttons default to "Show all."
- Be careful what you browse on a public or unsecured Wi-Fi network.
- Click on Account security to opt for e-mail alerts for infractions to your settings.
- Be aware that apps you use often have access to your Facebook information.
- Go through your options on the Privacy page to check that your friends don't give access via their programs to your Facebook page.
- Be aware of suspicious links.

*"A post I recommend you avoid: 'We took a Sharpie and wrote our names and hotel on our stomachs before we hit Bourbon Street in New Orleans for a night of partying.'"*

Do not use a public forum of social media to voice complaints, or shortly thereafter you will have to follow with an apology while nursing a damage-control headache. You may end up being called the bully. Disagree in a nice, not hateful or negative, way. You can openly discuss issues and express views while respecting others. Go offline when things get heated or when you are upset, angry, or drinking alcohol.

**ONLINE/OFFLINE: DIGITAL BULLIES AND BACKSTABBERS**

Four out of five of us will experience a coworker who tries to bully or backstab. In all walks of life there are people who suck time away in political maneuvering, grabbing resources, and creating distractions. These people can get your eyes watering:

- They secretly present your ideas as theirs.
- They take credit for your work to help them get ahead.
- They attempt character assassination.
- They provide you misleading information to their own benefit.
- They step over people, you included.
- They fabricate to try to save themselves.
- They endeavor to bring you down with disrespect.
- They create conflicts of interest.
- They try to trick you into badmouthing the company.
- They share private peer conversations.
- They go over your head and behind your back.
- They work to get your job away from you.
- They disassociate from you after you help them.
- They undermine you with micro-inequities, such as not returning phone calls and leaving you out of meetings, and generally make you feel, as one CEO put it, like "a sharpened instrument is being eased into the fleshy portion of your body."

Here's an example of the digital variations on bullying. Some employees were sending e-mails around badmouthing the boss, and they were doing so using the BCC e-mail option. One recipient took it upon himself to call a halt to it in an e-mail by hitting Reply all, which simultaneously exposed the people at fault.

Note: Bosses can and do bully when they instill fear in their employees by acting tyrannically, manipulatively, abusively, disrespectfully, condescendingly, or rudely. Sometimes they act in these ways themselves; sometimes they hire other people to do it for them. They are stupid to act this way as it will cause employees to not give their best and to cut and run the moment they can.

Always have your antenna up because bullying is omnipresent among human beings. Nevertheless, don't fight every fight with bullies, and don't try to win all the fights you pick.

Ask yourself:

- Is this important?
- Is my anger appropriate?
- Is my anger modifiable?
- Is this worth taking action?
- How do I see myself in this? (It's best to assess and confess to your contribution to the problem.)

When you answer those questions, you might wisely choose to ignore the situation. Sometimes it's not worth the time and action. But if you can't ignore it, then you have to directly and tactfully address the person and the situation.

So how do you stand up for yourself without belittling others? Play your hand privately at first. Learn what you can about the person. (Homeland Security experts say good intelligence prevents aggressive actions and prevents attacks.) Study how others interact and deal with the person: with respect, or do they merely tolerate? Understand that the person probably has been successfully backstabbing for years; she didn't start the poison with you.

Cyberspace bullying needs to be taken seriously:

- Don't reply to his posts, e-mails, or text messages. Your replying is what he wants because it makes him feel powerful.
- Don't reply with an emotional response because she will feel she is "getting to you."
- Don't delete his messages. Print them out as evidence.
- Report the incident to your manager; to your Internet, IM, or mobile phone provider; and to the police if necessary.
- Enlist friends and fans to take the same actions.

Dealing online or off, dig deep into your own thinking and come to terms with your desired outcome. In person: Prepare for an intervention (which may require several attempts). Being afraid to talk is cowardice.

Do not call out, confront, or attempt to embarrass the bully in public—despite how much you want to. Instead, invite the person to meet with you: "I'd like to meet you to talk. How about tomorrow?"

*"If you want to really knock 'em off balance, when you meet, walk over to him and say, 'Welcome, I'm glad you're here,' and give him a hug."*

### HOW THE BACKSTABBER CAN BENEFIT YOUR CAREER

Paradoxically, a backstabber can actually benefit your career. When a colleague causes an ugly confrontation and you're the one who resolves the issues, cleans up the messes, and gets everyone back on track, you'll be lauded as a true leader.

When your enemy draws negative attention to you but the attacker is proven wrong, you come out looking better than you did before the skirmish. The bad guy has just done you the favor of tooting your (positive) horn—and you didn't have to do it yourself.

Warfare keeps you on your toes. When you're under scrutiny, you focus harder on doing the right things all the time. You make more effort to be accountable and consistently above board in everything you do. You learn emotional self-defense when someone is trying to destroy you.

You also learn what *not* to do. Your attacker can be a "good model of bad behavior" that you don't want to emulate. When you see the backstabber or badmouther at work, you "walk in their Cole Hans" and become more aware of how your own actions can affect others. You also will be inspired to cut back on casual gossip, rein in any tendency to aggressively attack others, and handle your critiques of people differently and better. When someone is acting erratically, it becomes pretty easy for you to look good in comparison, especially when you act proactively, not just reactively.

Having an online or offline backstabber makes you focus on what is really important in your life and career. It builds zero tolerance for pettiness. You learn to embrace the complexity of human nature. As the attacker's vendettas fizzle, you better understand that backstabbers are insecure and threatened individuals; opportunistic and overly competitive to get ahead; and usually envious of you or resentful of something you've accomplished. They have pretty misdirected thinking, but when you observe it, you will learn not to be naïve to the ways of fellow human beings.

You build improved persuasion and presentation skills in reacting to these backstabbers. When someone else is trying to take credit for your work or disparage it, you learn a stronger way to speak up and speak out to tell your boss and company leaders about your accomplishments. Necessity is the mother of reinvention.

Having backstabbing colleagues is not a pleasant experience. However, people who get to the top are not afraid of conflict. They usually don't like it or start it—but they have developed the ability to focus on results over emotions, even when under attack.

The current employment climate can trigger bloodthirsty

behavior even in coworkers you've known and trusted. Scientists find when rats are in a cage and the heat is turned up under it, some of the rats start to bite the other rats. If it hasn't happened to you, it likely will. Accept the fact you'll have some sleepless nights experiencing corporate indigestion, but don't give up or back up. Survivalists train to endure, adapt, and overcome when confronted with a challenge. It's a good strategy for business obstacles too.

Keep your sense of humor, and remember, people will forget and go onto the next juicy gossip in the very near future.

## ONLINE COMMUNITIES ARE NOT A SUBSTITUTE FOR IN-PERSON HUMAN CONNECTIONS

Too many times, people like to think they are connecting because they are part of a back-and-forth discussion. But when the circumstances of the discussion protect the participants by giving them relative anonymity and the freedom to express without consequences, the discussion is spineless. For every half-hour you spend on an online site, you should put that same amount of time into being with other people in person.

The real test of your networking efforts is your ability to pick up the phone and actually get a person to talk to you. One Facebook fanatic invited his 500 friends to join up at a bar to test how many would. What would your guess be as to how many did? The answer is three. And those were the three people he had told about the experiment on the phone.

Have some no-electronics time. Give yourself and the people around you some digital white space. Studies have shown that the use of cell phones and computers one hour before sleep can interfere with normal sleep patterns. Another study showed that people who had a computer monitor in their bedroom had sex two times less often on average than those who didn't. And another documented that six hours a day sitting takes years off a person's life, increases waistlines, and lowers the level of good HDL cholesterol. Scientists have concluded that radiation from cell phones can potentially cause brain cancer, and they recommend you use a hands-free phone or at least keep the cell phone a few inches from your head.

*"You become so boring in person that by default it turns into a virtual relationship because the person you are dealing with is gone, and goes away to stay."*

You create unnecessary problems for yourself when:

- You get tethered to electronics at the cost of human contact. In turn, your interpersonal skills get rusty, and your social skills atrophy.
- You lose your gut feelings about people from the physical clues you hear in their voices or see in the whites of their eyes.
- Your gadget glows, rings, or sings, and it instantly grabs your attention. You become afraid of missing something.
- You can't get away from work because there are so many ways to reach you.
- You miss out on so much going on around you.

*"At 5:30 in the morning, I'm checking e-mail from Europe. By 8:30 that morning, I'm on a video chat in New York. At 10:30 at night, on a conference call with China . . . Even on vacation, people tracked me down at the pool through the hotel management, which they had to do because I had purposefully left my cell phone off."*

Get out; meet people. Stay in; meet people. Both are necessary to widen your circle of business friendships because they will become a part of your career. As you mix and mingle, exist and coexist, leaders will be needed—it's going to be someone, and it might as well be you.

*"I decided to get out of Facebook and get into somebody's face, but first I needed to get a facelift."*

You or someone over you will become the top dog, el Jefe, Mr. or Ms. Big, the Grand Poobah, numero uno, or the head honcho in charge of your team, project, organization, or company. That someone can influence and shape people, policy, industry, and even society online and offline. Again, why shouldn't it be you? You will read some stories in the next chapter from various top dogs and how they go about their work.

### WHAT'S IRRITATING ABOUT ONLINE COMMUNITIES?
When people:

- I don't know try to friend me or link in
- In the community distribute my personal information without my knowledge or approval
- Overshare, especially mundane details
- Are like stalkers, voyeurs; when they snoop around for information on me
- Fake online lives to impress others
- Use it as a tool to be rude and say things they wouldn't say in person
- Make passive-aggressive statements directed toward someone specific
- Tag my picture without my permission
- Use the online community instead of e-mail; when people have entire conversations on the site

- Use it as a soapbox
- Post comments that have grammatical errors and poor spelling
- Have hundreds of friends that they would never speak to in person
- Request a recommendation from me even though I have little history or it would be a negative one

# CHAPTER 5

## Users' Stories

As you know, my approach to learning is to talk with people to understand their experiences and gain new knowledge, creating one huge, global mentorship.

During this learning process, I spoke with many people whose stories deserved their own space in this book. I asked a diverse group to write with this direction: "Tell the readers the story of your experience in utilizing technology. Give them a takeaway that will help them in their careers."

It was broad, general direction, and from it, some absolutely wonderful stories came out to me. See if you don't agree.

### ALLISON SALTZER, MICROSOFT

Former companies: Arthur Andersen, Qwest Communications, and JD Edwards. Husband: CEO of an all-natural foods company. Has traveled the world. Sang on stage with the Beach Boys. Two children. Hobbies: skiing, camping, biking, and hiking. Favorite saying: It's better than perfect. It's DONE.

Some time back I worked with a tall thin man who is about six feet, four inches. When he's in front of a room, he has a large, charismatic presence. Most of his interactions with his sales team are virtual since his territory covers a large portion of the United States. He does a great job of using videoconferencing whenever he has an all-hands call. But he has never optimized his office to use his video in the most flattering manner.

First, the lighting is not ideal—he has a large window behind him, so he appears very much in the shadows when videoconferencing. Second, he hasn't given much thought to how he appears. While I'm sure he goes to the men's room to straighten his shirt before our meetings, he uses the webcam on his small laptop and its mic, and he spends the entire call bent over looking like some praying mantis. Instead of a commanding, confident appearance, he looks uncomfortable and awkward—not the right impression for an executive.

I am very fortunate that I get to work from home most days. While my luck for the convenience of working from home makes me grateful, I also realize I need to do even more to stand out. There are a few things I do to make sure I make an excellent impression, even when I'm not there in person:

1. **High quality video camera**: I've invested in the best one there is—a high-definition (HD), light-sensitive camera. I've maximized where I've mounted it on my monitor, and following the advice of my friend in film directing, I keep it about 20 degrees above me so it is slightly looking down. That's apparently the most flattering angle, as compared to most people who have their camera on their laptop, causing them to hunch over.

2. **Lighting**: I tested my video camera and realized that when my window is open and it's daylight, the entire right side of my face is washed out. The best light is when I pull my shades and turn my office light on.

3. **Dress**: While I'm in my workout clothes most days, I keep a black blazer, necklace, hairband, and lipstick close to my

monitor. That way if someone wants to have a videoconference, I look professional in the blink of an eye.

4. **Microphone**: I've maximized my hardware at home and tested everything. I realized that my microphone on my video camera picked up all kind of ambient noise like my aquarium. Now I use my VoIP headset—I look a little like a *Time/Life* operator, but I know that people can hear me clearly.

5. **Background**: I consciously created the backdrop of my video with two green plants on either side of me and an inviting painting of a window. It looks professional, yet inviting. My boss said, "I really like your setup on video. It makes me want to step into your office. It almost looks staged!" I turned to him and said, "Dewa, of COURSE it's staged!!"

### WHEN THE STAKES ARE HIGH

I was interviewing for my dream job. Unfortunately, the rounds of interviews were all virtual, so I needed to make sure my video setup was top notch. I tested all of the conference rooms in the office, and I found the one with the best lighting. When I set up my camera, I realized that I needed some items to prop it up.

I got several boxes from the mailroom and stacked them so they appeared stable. When I tested my camera, I found that the painting and the clock behind me were distracting, so I took them off the wall. Anyone looking into the office would have thought that someone was moving! But via video camera, I looked prepared and centered, with no distractions.

### MY SECRETS TO REMOTE WORK

Build deep relationships face-to-face—especially when starting: I've found that by scheduling a regular travel cadence (especially when first beginning a new role), I can quickly build a deep, trusted relationship. Why? Not only do I make maximum use of meeting time but I also schedule lunches and dinners with appropriate stakeholders and coworkers. I've found that since I come in from out of town, people make time for more off-hours interaction.

The conversations and personal bonds you make outside of the office are often much deeper than the five-minute "water cooler" interactions. This allows for easier work relationships and more creative thinking, since you connect on a more personal level and can get deeper insight into what's important to each stakeholder.

I make maximum use of the technology available. I've optimized my home office to use webcams and Lync technologies on a daily basis. This includes considerations for lighting and connectivity. Even if other people are not as comfortable with webcams as I am, I use mine so they feel as though there is a closer connection. I also regularly share my desktop so collaboration is in real time and easy.

Provide regular status updates outside of one-to-one time. One of the keys to working successfully remotely is being "visible" even when you aren't visible. Written status updates outside of "normal" one-to-ones help managers feel as though you are on top of things. Including next steps and gating factors (with solutions) give visibility into work that is often more comprehensive than is possible in casual conversations in person.

Understand others' work cadence and preferred hours. I support the northwest district, which is an hour behind mountain standard time. For all of my sales managers and strategic service delivery partners (SSPs), I discuss their preferred times for interaction. Some people are early birds (as I am) and like to meet early in the morning during their most productive time of day. Others have long commutes where what is typically downtime can be turned into valuable productive time for off-hours interaction. Others prefer conversing later in the evening.

By approaching a flexible work schedule, where I can maximize interaction based on others' preferences and availability, I can mitigate time zone challenges.

For example, a former manager had a one-hour commute in the morning, so we always scheduled our one-to-ones during that time—she appreciated utilizing her downtime, and I got more focused attention without the multitasking that often happens when someone is in her office. One of my sales managers now takes the ferry to work, and we have fun and funny conversations, not only about work challenges and opportunities but also about the seagulls in the distance. This setup, again, creates a personal bond that is atypical.

Rather than "work-life balance," I am a huge proponent of a work-life *blend*. The difference is having a fluid, flexible approach with which you make time for the important things, both work and family. I am connected even when I'm not connected.

Use the phone: *a lot*. Instead of e-mail threads that can go back and forth multiple times, whenever possible I pick up the phone. This is more efficient, and again, it creates a personal relationship.

Be excellent. When people see your results and the way you approach your work, excellence supersedes *presence* every time. Following up, doing what you say you're going to do, and staying on top of next steps and relationships promotes that perception of excellence.

**BARRY LENSON, AUTHOR**

Former companies: Trump Entrepreneur Initiative (formerly Trump University) and the National Institute of Business Management (NIBM). Has written or coauthored a dozen books including the Amazon.com bestseller *Good Stress, Bad Stress*. Earned two black belts in Jujitsu. Earned degrees in voice and opera and sang professionally until his early thirties. One daughter. Swims and attends classical music concerts and plays. Favorite saying: Most of what delights the world is just a brief dream.

This is the story of my father's digital ever after.

My father, the painter Michael Lenson, died back in 1971. That was long before the Internet was even the proverbial twinkle in anyone's eye. Yet the Internet has played a major role in what could be called my father's digital afterlife, a period in which his reputation and renown have grown dramatically.

Back in June 2001, I built www.michaellenson.org, a website about him and his work. I can't recall exactly what my motivation was. I had all kinds of documents about his life and work—his résumé, a bibliography of books and magazines that mentioned him, a list of museums that owned his work. And of course, I had lots of images of his paintings. I figured, why not put all that material up on a website instead of letting it sit in my files where nobody but me could see it?

In the decade since then, the website has delivered returns that are nothing short of staggering. But before I describe what those benefits have been, I want to state a few facts clearly.

The website I created was nothing extravagant. Instead of hiring a designer, I built it using the not-very-elegant templates that the hosting service provided. I never gave a thought to optimizing the website by using key terms that would attract visitors. I don't update the content on the website very often, which is something that all the Internet gurus say is imperative if you want a site that will attract visitors. I have never used pay-per-click advertising to bring visitors to the site. I have hardly ever embedded links to other sites, and I have never started to blog about my father or his work.

So, what I am saying is, I built a site that is a hedgehog in comparison to all the high-performing sites out there. But as I am about to tell you, it has returned so many benefits that I would like to place a candle in front of its landing page, bow my head, and offer it my most profound thanks. Let me tell you what some of those benefits have been.

First, the site has been critically important in getting my father's work mentioned in dozens of magazines and books. Authors and publishers have discovered my dad through the site, and they have used images of his work as book covers and illustrations. Authors have found out about him, then mentioned him in articles and books about the history of American art. The most notable of these was the historian Nick Taylor, who discovered my father's website and used him as a major case history in the book *American Made: The Enduring Legacy of the WPA*. (My father was head of the mural projects in New Jersey in the 1930s under the auspices of the Works Progress Administration [WPA], and he painted major murals around the state.) But there have been other important things written about my father too, thanks to the site. In 2011, he was the subject of a feature article in *DesignNJ*, a glossy New Jersey monthly. (That's just one example of many.)

Second, the site has led galleries and museums to discover my father's work. Several years ago, an art gallery in Philadelphia found out about my father through his website, and it presented a one-man show of his work. And I have gotten many inquiries from dealers who have gone on to represent his work.

Third, the site has helped me discover a large body of my father's work. Nearly every month, I get an inquiry from someone who owns a painting of my dad's and who wants to know more about him. Often, I am able to obtain images of these works for my records. Sometimes these discoveries are amazing. In the summer of 2011 thanks to the website, I acquired a painting that my father had painted in Paris in 1931, during his years of study there. An art dealer in Tennessee found it, contacted me about it through the site, and I bought it from him. How a painting of my dad's got from Paris to Tennessee is the kind of mystery that any artist's son likes.

Fourth, the website has provided some astonishing coincidences, many of which have enriched my knowledge of my father and his work. One of these coincidences is so remarkable that I want to describe it here at a little more length.

Back in the 1930s when my father was studying in Paris, he painted a stunning portrait of Henrietta Schumann, an American concert pianist who was studying there at the same time. I only had a photograph of this painting in my files and a copy of an article about it that appeared in *Town & Country* magazine in 1929. Before I built the website, my attempts to find the painting were unsuccessful.

I spent a day at the New York Public Library back around 1983, and I found out that after coming back to America, Schumann had embarked on a major concert career and appeared in recitals with major orchestras. But she had died suddenly in 1949, at the age of 39. Her obituary in the *New York Times* reported that she was married to a man named Thomas H. Barker, that she had lived in Gladwyne, a small town in Pennsylvania, and that she had left behind a daughter named Bonnie.

Armed with that info, I attempted unsuccessfully to find anyone named Barker in Pennsylvania. I tried to find someone named Bonnie Barker living anywhere in America. No luck. But then in 2008, pretty much on a whim, I put an image of the portrait on my father's website and asked if anyone had any information about it. About two weeks later, Bonnie was sitting in her home in Virginia with a friend, who looked at a drawing by my father that was hanging on the wall and said, "Don't you want to investigate a bit about that artist?"

So Bonnie Googled my father's name, landed on my home page, and saw the portrait of her mother there. It had been nearly 70 *years* since her mother had last seen my father. But thanks to the Internet, those years disappeared in a moment. Unfortunately, Bonnie does not own that elusive portrait, but she owns several other works by my dad. Since then, she and I have become friends.

She even sent me an envelope of photographs of my father that were taken in Paris around 1930. I scanned them, and I put some up on the site. I am sure that other surprises lie ahead too, though probably nothing as breathtaking as that one.

Would my father's work be known if I had never created that website for him? Undoubtedly. But undoubtedly too, his reputation as an important American painter would not be as strong as it is now. I am about to set up a Facebook page for my dad too, but my immediate advice to you is, have a website. Just do it. In ways you can never predict or control, it has the ability to work true miracles in your life. I know it did for my dad. Why couldn't it do the same for you too?

### REAR ADMIRAL HAROLD "HAL" PITTMAN, U.S. NAVY

Deputy chief of staff for communication, reporting to the commander of the International Security Assistance Force (ISAF), Kabul, Afghanistan. Responsible for all public affairs and information operations in Afghanistan, as well as integrated communication planning and liaison activities with related Afghan ministries and NATO Coalition partner nations. Enlisted in the Navy as a journalist. An award-winning writer. Three sons. Hobbies: reading, writing, working out, and coaching his sons in numerous sports. Favorite saying: "Nothing in the world can take the place of persistence. Talent will not; nothing is more common than unsuccessful men with talent. Genius will not; unrewarded genius is almost a proverb. Education will not; the world is full of educated derelicts. Persistence and determination alone are omnipotent." —Calvin Coolidge, thirtieth president of the United States

I'm writing about "any day in Afghanistan . . . ."

My alarm clock and BlackBerry go off simultaneously; I turn

on the light, check the BlackBerry for overnight e-mails, and prepare for another day leading the NATO International Security Assistance Force's communication efforts in Afghanistan.

I've been wearing the uniform of the United States Navy for nearly 29 years now. As a public affairs officer, I have worked in media and information for most of my career, and as a Navy rear admiral, I have been fortunate to continue to receive promotions in a traditionally small and specialized military career field.

Since the early 1990s, I've spent a considerable amount of time in the Middle East and Central Asia, and being at the apex of the field has afforded me the opportunity to deploy and serve my country in Afghanistan at an important time in U.S. history.

I lead the communication efforts of a 49-nation coalition. Our functions include media relations and social media engagement, strategic communication planning, and production of Afghan television and radio spots and billboards.

I also serve as the International Security Assistance Force's (ISAF's) strategic partner for three Afghan ministries and the Afghan Olympic Committee through my Traditional Communication division: military members assisting Afghans through people-to-people programs like facilitating youth *shuras* and helping develop community-based, sustainable youth sports to create alternative opportunities for Afghan kids. I also serve as a liaison with spokespersons for the security-related ministries, spokesperson for the president, and the director of the Government Media Information Center.

Our communication tools range from social media to old-school word-of-mouth. On our organizational website, we use social media—Facebook, Flickr, Twitter, and YouTube—run by a small social media team, and we review social media trends and analyze U.S. and international sites in our daily media analysis and assessment. While fewer than 10 percent of Afghans have access to the web today, we know that figure is quickly increasing. We push to shape the communication environment using technology that may seem simplistic elsewhere. But here it's a challenging, dynamic war zone requiring military know-how and ingenuity, political awareness, and diplomatic savvy to move things forward little by little. The Internet is also still a critical outlet for reaching other important audiences and the public through the media, the elites, the Diaspora, and various troop-contributing nations.

Cell phone use has exploded across the country since the fall of the Taliban in 2001, and since cell phones are an important tool for public communication, we use text/SMS messaging to communicate with Afghans. My team is involved in facilitating the expansion of cell phone infrastructure, and we're also working with other U.S. organizations on an infrastructure program designed to expand the footprint of radio and television. The thought here is that greater access to public information increases the decision-making abilities of the people and increases their voice in this fledgling democracy, even as we seek to limit the Taliban's use of communication systems to maximize their propaganda. Add to that idea the nuance of operating in a pressurized, hostile environment, where one could be shot at—and it's clearly enough to fill one's day.

Before breakfast, I check the three different e-mail systems in my room (different classification levels), shower, don my uniform, and walk three minutes to the office. I have a yogurt with coffee, and I hold my first meeting by 6:45 a.m. to review communication issues of the day, including breaking news stories, media assessment, and upcoming public communication events, like national media embeds and interviews.

This information will shortly be briefed via PowerPoint to the four-star general who runs NATO military operations in Afghanistan, along with the senior multinational staff, so the 6:45 pre-brief is my opportunity to review our team's public communication snapshot for the next 72 hours.

The commander's early morning standup brief by secure video teleconference reaches every headquarters in the 130,000-person multinational team, as well as sites in Europe and the United States. It is a forum for information exchange among leaders, and it is an opportunity for the commander to articulate guidance. Simultaneously, slides for today's brief and links to ongoing tactical events populate a full wall of information, and the public communication, public diplomacy, and information operations functional area is always a key topic of discussion.

At midmorning, I hold my internal communication staff standup from a conference room adjacent my office. This is a fast exchange with outstations via spider phone. We discuss the tactics of the day's communication efforts and how we will keep Washington, NATO, and our chains of command informed.

We try to start the meeting with five minutes of discussion on communication planning or other discreet efforts. This meeting sometimes devolves to discussions of tactical actions, but that is because the communications effort at a strategic headquarters still includes tactical, day-to-day elements like media relations. At this meeting, we may discuss media embeds with operating forces, responses to breaking news issues, ongoing Afghan government activities, strategic communication planning initiatives or briefings, and efforts in conjunction with colleagues at the U.S. embassy, the office of the senior civilian representative to NATO, and an array of nongovernmental organizations.

It's easy to get bogged down in detail, but my job is about focusing on the big strategic issues that could influence the narrative in Afghanistan, among troop contributing nations, or back in Washington. It is an inherently political environment, and the enemy—Al Qaeda, the Taliban, and the various insurgent groups allied with them—gets a vote.

This undertaking was even more daunting before the NATO force developed the right organization (just a couple of years ago) to fight and win against an insurgency. Our headquarters communication operation is decentralized, but I do have a robust team to ensure that we can mass effort on problems quickly. Our operations are 24/7, and the team works seven days a week to message those operations, strategize, plan, and respond to an ever-present lineup of global media challenges. The deployment is six months in the combat zone for some, a year for others; I'll serve just over a year.

About half the time, I take lunch at my desk. My calendar can become stacked with back-to-back meetings and briefings, and lunch is the white space that allows me to catch up on my three e-mail systems, read, plan, and think. Of course, there are also two phones and a Tandberg video teleconference system on my desk, which means I never quite unplug—whether I am reading a 20-page plan, editing broadcast public service announcement scripts, or touching up talking points for the next media or key leader engagement.

It's a war, and as the senior communicator, you never run out of crises. I prioritize and reprioritize throughout the day, balancing time zones (we're three and a half hours ahead of Europe and NATO, and eight and a half hours ahead of the Pentagon).

By midafternoon, the e-mails and telephone calls from Washington begin to hit. I usually conduct product reviews in the afternoon, where I see some of our more sensitive operational efforts, and I'll do a closeout standup with my senior executive team late in the afternoon. It is a multinational leadership team, with a Canadian deputy, British information operations chief, German spokesperson, and American public affairs chief. They are a "captive audience," and regardless of our close-of-business standup time, I'm still able to reach them at their desks until 9 or 10 p.m.—meaning that a 5:30 p.m. closeout enables the team a chance to get dinner and a workout and still put in a couple more hours of work before bedtime!

As for me, sometimes the evening routine is dinner with a minister, deputy minister, or Afghan official. In traditional societies like Afghanistan, face-to-face communication over a meal or cup of tea is often the best way to get the job done. It might be at an official's residence or at a restaurant, or even on the NATO compound. Whenever I attend these, I'm accompanied by my translator and cultural advisor, in addition to one or two action officers, who, at the end of the day, will be tasked with carrying out the programs we're discussing.

The only women who attend these dinners are from my team, and we try hard to be culturally astute. Even in such traditional a society, I'm surprised if officials don't check their BlackBerrys once or twice during the evening—the electronic leash is everywhere.

Other evenings, I'll hit the gym for an hour-long workout. I've been working out for 35 years now, and that hour provides time to think through the events of the day, and activities for tomorrow.

By 11 p.m., I'm back in my room, which is steps from the operations center. If there's a spare second, I may try to read.

I'll also try to squeeze in a call to my wife Rebecca and 12-year-old son via Skype; while we exchange e-mail during the day, there is nothing quite like a familiar voice on the other end of the phone—er, headset. Then I quickly check my own Facebook and LinkedIn pages, and I make one last check of my three business e-mail systems, set the clock and BlackBerry, and it's time for a couple of hours of sleep. . . until tomorrow, when I'll do it all again with a new set of challenges.

### BRANDON AKI, BRANDONAKI CONSULTING

Courtship consultant. Air Force Academy graduate. Jet pilot for the Air Force. Spent years competing as a fencer. Hobbies: poker and chess.

Favorite saying: Who you were has made you who you are today, but who you were can never dictate what you can become.

Along my path in life I have had a number of different names, ranks, and designations, but the title I wear most proudly is CEO.

I served for more than a decade in the Air Force, and the training prepared me for a myriad of difficult situations that have helped me meet the demands of becoming a CEO—no less than 100 percent effort each day. I worked long hours, researched my craft, surrounded myself by great mentors, and relied on their advice to help me navigate the treacherous journey of an entrepreneur.

My time as a pilot taught me that the fastest path toward gaining knowledge is to first understand where you are and then focus on where you want to be. What I wasn't prepared for were the miles of uncharted territory that life in the rapidly changing, digital world would present.

Where I was: I had a message, and there were people who wanted to hear it. Where I wanted to be: In a place where my reach and influence could capture a large percentage of a relatively untapped market. It would eventually take a careful mixture of introspection and a constant ability to adapt to a changing environment to go from aviator and military officer to courtship consultant. At the end of the day, success for my company meant having a steady stream of clients and advice that they could call upon at any moment. I decided to start by doing small, in-person seminars.

The seminars were broken down into multiple sessions and were intended to grow by word-of-mouth. I followed those up with blogs on various hot topics that were on the collective minds of my clients. Clients could view these blogs online, they received e-mail alerts when they were posted, and they could subscribe to them via RSS feed.

The results were better than expected. New potential clients started following my blog, they interacted with each other on posts, and my local clientele began to grow. I was then able to fine-tune my approach and concentrate on a particular niche. One day an attendee at one of my seminars decided to call into a nationally syndicated radio show to tell them about my work. I was eventually invited to appear on the radio show, but in the process I was faced with a new challenge. I needed to find a way to direct national radio listeners to my blog and eventually convert a percentage of them into clients. I decided to create a website.

Having a well-thought-out and content-driven website is no longer a luxury. It is a necessity. My website had to help potential customers understand who I was, what I believe in, and what I could do for them. It had to accurately regulate the flow of information from the radio and my blog. It also had to help people properly understand me as a brand, and it had to act as a hub of information that would guide outsiders down a specific path to becoming clients. But, like technology, I had to continue evolving. My multipage weekly blog, along with an increasing client workload, was getting my business great exposure, but it was also becoming time-consuming.

I began researching other ways to get a tighter, more compact message out to my followers. I knew I needed to promulgate my message on a daily basis, so after months of rebelling against social media, I decided to embrace it and incorporate Facebook, Twitter, and Tumblr into my site. The social media component proved to be an invaluable addition to my business because it took a revealed preference (the way in which individuals had expressed their preferences for receiving information online), and it used that particular medium to communicate my common themes to them each day.

A critical shift in the way I was interacting with potential clients was taking place. Word-of-mouth was leading them, digitally, through one of my online components. When potential clients decided that they wanted to learn more about me, they would follow a link to my website and apply for my program. I was then able to conduct one-on-one consults, and since they already had a good idea about my personality and how I could help them, my conversion rates were higher and my daily workload decreased.

I began receiving even more national exposure. I was featured in *Marie Claire* magazine and various other online magazines, and I am now exploring offers in television. However, it's hard to understand the impact of particular types of exposure unless you have the means to measure it. I did research and decided to start using an analytics tool to monitor traffic to and from my website. The amount of information I was able to gather was tremendous.

People were visiting my website from the United States and a number of different countries, but the numbers of individuals who were applying for my program weren't increasing at a proportional rate. I had to figure out how to not only get people to come to my website but also how to give them a reason to keep coming back for more. In addition, I had to figure out how to expand my message to international users without physically being in their countries.

My frequent flyer miles began piling up, but I also decided to incorporate video chat capability into my arsenal of business tools. I began feeding YouTube and other video interviews into my site—now people could not only read the words in my blog and social media but they could also see my face. These elements were then fed directly into my website, and, soon, people could simply save my site as a bookmark and visit it every day for advice on dating.

The Internet, online resources, and social media are changing our world and business, and they are changing the way we interact with each other on a daily basis. I attribute the success of my company to the fact that I was able to open my mind to the possibilities the online world has to offer. As a CEO in a rapidly changing digital world, we must constantly stay ahead in order to keep up.

### SONIA MARRERO, COVIDIEN SURGICAL SOLUTIONS

Principal project engineer. Also worked at Maxtor, now part of Seagate Technology. Born in Puerto Rico. Fluent in English and Spanish. Coauthor of U.S. Patent 7757378. One son: Hunter Marrero. Hobbies: tennis and taking scenic walks. Favorite saying: Be genuine.

Debra asked contributors for interesting, effective ways to use mobile devices, videos, and social media. As I was giving it some thought, I started thinking about some of the key elements that one would need to consider when trying to make a decision on what type of media to use to reach an unconventional goal. Here are some key elements of that decision-making process:

1. Have you recently used one of the common mass media venues (including mobile devices, video, e-mail, and/or social media) to reach an unconventional goal? If so, what was the venue and intended message?

2. How did you determine the type of venue that you would use?

The venue selection could vary depending on the type of message that is to be delivered. For example, executive management could use global corporate e-mails as fast delivery venues for employees within their company. With the rise of global and international business structures, key messages that would have been delivered in person are now e-mailed to employees. Topics range from plant accomplishments to major organizational changes.

A marketing firm contracted to promote a specific product or service may choose to attend a trade show and invite key customers with the use of a postcard and an invitation to their hospitality suite. This is different from an MP3 player targeted to be sold to younger adults, which could be posted on a social network with a coupon with which youngsters could quickly access the information. You could also link a prize to completion of an e-mail survey. Some companies have gone as far as asking employees to complete health surveys that provide insight into the health insurance projections in exchange for lower health insurance premiums. In this case, this is a mutually beneficial situation in which the company obtains data that it needs and the employee gets something in return that is very tangible.

3. What were the driving factors to use that type of venue (cost, accessibility to others, outreach potential, list of intended recipients, and so on)?

When trying to work through the decision, you need to consider the breadth of the reach that you are intending for the message. E-mail communications are relatively inexpensive if the distribution lists exist. When using e-mail, you need to have the correct distribution list. You don't want to abuse the communication lines that are open within your network. The message has to benefit the recipients in such a way that they will continue to read your messages.

If you intend to reach certain demographics that may not use digital media, a paper mailing may be more appropriate. If you go with a paper mailing, the message must be condensed to ensure that all information fits within the smallest size possible such as a postcard.

4. In your opinion, was the venue effective based on the outcome or response?

The effectiveness should be measured by a metric such as a follow-up survey, increase in sales, attendance at a function, or direct feedback.

5. If you had to do it again, what would you change or improve?

Once you try to use a specific venue, you should go back and document lessons learned based on the previous experience. This should include all aspects of the delivery: venue, cost, distribution lists, and results.

### SCOTT REGAN, APIGEE
Chief marketing officer. Former companies: Accenture, Microsoft, BEA, and Yahoo!. Commutes to work on a bike daily. Two children. Hobbies: skiing, guitar, surfing, and biking. Favorite saying: We always overestimate the change that will occur in the next 2 years but always underestimate the change that will occur in the next 10.

Are you a business executive trying to understand if, when, and how to go about getting involved with social networking? Here are 10 thoughts on starting that process.

### 1. ENGAGE
Social networks are here to stay as important channels via which you as an executive can connect with peers, customers, prospects, and friends. Utilizing these online connections won't be optional for either you or your company much longer.

Imagine if you hadn't tried the web by 1998—that's where you are if you haven't started to build your social networking executive presence by now.

## 2. KNOW YOUR NETWORK

Each social network serves a slightly different purpose and has a different protocol. You need to understand them to be effective. For example, LinkedIn is for professional networking. Once you create your professional profile page—think of it as your online résumé—you add your business contacts to your network. You can then ask to be introduced to other executives through your network contacts, or other executives might reach out to you through your network. You can also join online professional groups in areas of interest or expertise. When you're on LinkedIn, you present yourself in the same way that you might at a first business meeting with an important client or potential boss.

Some LinkedIn tips:

- Make sure your experience profile—which is now effectively your résumé—is up to date and accurate.
- Want headhunters to find you? Use words in your résumé that they might use to find ideal candidates.
- Whenever you make a change to your profile (changing your photo, adding a new section of experience), the change goes out in a newsletter. Know that people might think you're "updating your résumé looking for a new job."

Twitter is a public forum, where you are broadcasting short 140-character updates (called "tweets") that are available for anyone to see, or fielding questions and comments from everyone (in your professional context, these are customers, clients, and prospects).

Here you create short updates that are visible for anyone to view, and anyone can follow you to view your updates. It's a great place to follow news from any publisher—from the *New York Times* to your favorite blogger or friend.

For professionals, Twitter is an increasingly important place to listen to customers. Customers or prospects may "tweet at you" (put your Twitter name, called a "handle" and referred to with an @ sign, such as @debrabenton). When customers tweet at you with a comment, compliment, or complaint, anyone can see that tweet (including your colleagues and boss), so you should acknowledge it (or they may start tweeting at your CEO!).

Some Twitter tips:

- You can be construed as a company spokesperson, whether you intend to or not.
- If your company already has a Twitter page or @handle, it's not a bad idea to check with the "official company tweeters" before publishing your own tweets referencing the company name.
- If your company doesn't yet have a Twitter handle such as @yourcompanyname, advocate that someone reserve than name and start monitoring it.
- You don't have to tweet to participate—Twitter needs listeners too! You can subscribe to updates and/or search for updates that mention your company or topics of interest. In fact, it's best to "listen" for a while to get the hang of it before jumping in.

Facebook is for networking with your friends. Your posts on Facebook are supposed to be private between you, your friends, and family. However, as your network grows, it becomes an increasingly likely possibility that someone in your professional life may see your personal posts, comments, photos, or other information through a friend of a friend. (After all, it's a small world in many industries.)

It may be a good practice to ask yourself what the implications would be if something you posted on Facebook found its way into your professional life. A picture of a sunset? No problem. College drinking photos? Maybe they don't belong on Facebook. Your high school hairdo? Your call.

### 3. *LISTEN FOR A WHILE*

Just as in many social situations, it's often a great idea to listen for a while (by following others' posts) to get a sense of context, personalities, protocols, and social norms before posting. This can be important if you are new to a social network or if you are an executive or professional representing your company and colleagues.

### 4. *KEEP IT ACTIVE*

If you decide to start participating in a social network, don't go weeks or months without a post. If your intention is to use social networking for professional purposes—interacting with customers or expressing a point of view—you might be giving the same impression as an empty storefront if you are not providing information often enough.

### 5. *BUT DON'T OVERDO IT*

A recent study showed that millionaires who actively participate in social networking spend less time than most other users on social networks. That makes sense—they're busy! Don't overdo it. Dozens of posts a day can create an impression that you don't have much else to do except for spend time on social networks!

### 6. *MAKE IT USEFUL*

It's not the quantity but the quality of participation. If you're going to put something out in a social network, try to make it a post or comment of value. Think about it from the perspective of the audience. If they are following your posts because you're an industry leader, they expect a perspective reflecting your experience and vantage point.

You can think of social networking as marketing—both marketing of your own personal brand and your company brand. Like all good marketing, if you want good results—make it about the audience, not you. Offer a point of view or call out items that are of interest and add some value. For example, share an article or a video interview of something that calls out an industry trend—it will be more interesting and valuable for your audience than when every post is about you or your company.

### 7. SHOWCASE YOUR NICHE AND EXPERTISE

How do you go about gaining a following? There are millions of people participating in social networks like Twitter. And most professional networks number in at least the hundreds of thousands. Why should someone follow you? What is your specific area of expertise that could make your posts valuable or stand out?

One reason people might follow you is because of the people that you follow—or that you are associated with. So it's not all about what you say. It's about whom you think is important to be listening to.

### 8. REMEMBER, YOU'RE BEING WATCHED

Always understand how widely your posts are distributed. On a public network like Twitter, anyone can see your conversations with a customer, colleague, or friend. Even "private" messages are sometimes accidentally exposed with only a misplaced character. If you are an executive or professional, know that reporters and bloggers may take any of your statements or commentary as being from your company.

**Tip**: Remember that your competitors are also watching! Don't tweet about a great meeting with prospects if you don't want your competitor calling them the next day.

**Tip**: Watch your competitors! If they tweet about a great meeting with prospects, call them the next day!

### 9. USE IT TO REINFORCE OFFLINE (REAL) RELATIONSHIPS

Social networking is often most effective when used as a way to reinforce and build on your real relationships. One of the best ways to use it is to keep a conversation going after a great meeting or conference.

### 10. KNOW WHEN TO KEEP IT IN YOUR PANTS

Your smart phone, that is.

The mark of great executives or professionals is often that they are present—in the moment, with their full attention to the conversation or decision at hand. When you detach from a conversation to attend to social networking (or any other action on your smart phone or laptop), you send the implicit message that you have left the moment and the current place and that there is somewhere else you would rather or need to be.

So when you can—keep that smart phone in your pants!

**TARAH KEECH, CONSULTANT**
Former companies: TeleVox Software, Washington Mutual, AT&T, and Victoria's Secret. Is an Air Force brat whose hobbies include spending time with her husband, cooking, shopping at farmers' markets, hosting small dinner parties, writing her blog stylepsychology.blogspot.com, and collecting words. Favorite saying: Want it? Ask for it.

Online job searching is painful. It can be intimidating, even downright discouraging, and it still makes my brow furrow when I think about it. All of those lonely hours spent scouring the expanse of the web and putting the best possible representation of myself out into the ether—freely offering up my greatest accomplishments and achievements for judgment.

Often I would not receive the smallest of indications that a human had even seen my résumé. Like one of my dad's favorite recollections of his childhood walks to school: it's a steep uphill climb, both ways, in the snow, alone. There are technological approaches that can help the search, and for me, there were three things that really made a difference.

First, use the extensive job board listings as a resource for your own research. When I began to look at jobs, I started first by looking at my possible "dream jobs." These postings were beyond my present qualifications (way beyond) but within my long-term view of possibility. I saw CEO and COO postings and began to imagine myself in those roles. From these postings I began a collage of sorts and started to identify themes in what they were looking for. Working backward, it became clearer how I could connect the dots to get myself into my very own C-suite. Studying the desired backgrounds for COOs, I could see that there was a theme of program directorship.

How does one qualify for program directorship? Program and project management. Well, I'll be. I have project and program leadership experience. Next, looking at project management jobs, I saw that they often referenced a preference for Project Management Professional (PMP) certification. I took the courses online, passed the test, and added the PMP certification as a tag to all of my online profiles and résumés. That is when the recruiters started calling and ultimately how I landed my current job.

Second, early on I began to use LinkedIn.com to accumulate a list of publicly accessible written recommendations. It is so simple—I wrote a dozen, sincere, one-paragraph recommendations for the people from whom I wanted a reciprocal recommendation and signed it with a request that they return the favor. Boom! Now, every letter of inquiry, cover letter, and résumé I send out points the reader directly back to my page where they can get an idea of the caliber of work I deliver and hear from "the horse's mouth" what my former coworkers and supervisors have to say about me.

Certainly, it is expected that when a job is offered, further references will be gathered, but I have heard from two separate recruiters that they were glad to see the recommendations and that they gave them an added vote of confidence when reaching out to me.

One note for consideration is to choose your recommendation requests carefully. A former colleague wrote nicely about my work with his firm, but then he elaborated, rather extensively, about his discontent with the company and one of our superiors. Lesson learned the hard way: You have to be judicious about soliciting feedback. Ultimately, I had to delete his contribution and deal with the discomfort of explaining why.

Another huge asset was having my résumé reviewed electronically by friends and strangers alike. Friendly perspectives can help you see your screen presence with more clarity, especially after you have looked at it for hours and the white space turns to static-wavy lines. Strangers, on the other hand, are amazing content critics.

If you're lucky enough to connect with recruiters post-rejection, ask them how your résumé reads and what content caught their eye and can be improved. The most valuable feedback I have ever gotten is when I roped in connections in my network that were at least two degrees removed. My best girlfriend's father-in-law is a highly successful businessperson. So much so, in fact, that now as a consultant in his retirement, he is grossing triple what he earned before because his expertise and experience are so immensely valued.

Prior to this exercise, this gentleman and I had only interacted superficially at two or three social events so he knew that I was a friend of the family, but he had no idea what I did or what I wanted out of my career—only slightly more familiar than a stranger. I e-mailed my friend and begged her to ask her dad-in-law to give my résumé a quick read and to please provide some direction on how to get noticed. I thought having the résumé read by a person who was not familiar with me but who was more like the executive player I wanted to be would be beneficial.

I tell you what: asking for unbiased feedback is not for the faint of heart. He was so generous with his review and track-changes that my résumé looked as though it had been run over by a train. Once I regained my pulse and consoled my ego, I looked objectively at his comments and did my best to address every concern and implement every suggestion.

Even when using a third-party agency for résumé rewrites (which I did straight out of grad school), you cannot get that level of feedback. He let me know how my presentation read to high-level executives and how to optimize my presentation to get my foot in the door. Now my résumé is much stronger, and so am I.

I acknowledge that job searching in this technological age is hard work. To maintain my optimism (and sanity), I force myself to remember that it is one of my life's highest callings. In order to measure up to the fullest potential of my life and career, I need to be in my dream job. To get that job I have to leverage technology. Doing so also serves as an opportunity to practice and expand the fullest measure of my work ethic, organizational skills, and networking abilities.

**MARKUS SCHWEIG, CIO WHISPERER**

Former companies: En Masse Entertainment, Smith & Tinnker, Hidden City Games, UniSpheres, Microsoft, and Siemens. At Microsoft, built the Xbox Operations Center and supported the infrastructure for the first 1 million online gamers in 19 countries. Survived sitting in a Boeing 737 when both of its engines stopped working at cruising altitude in the middle of the night. Hobbies: music, movies, online gaming, hiking, biking, and groundbreaking technologies that change the world for the better. Favorite saying: Imagine a better world and then create it. Do not forget to help someone every day along the way.

The emergence of virtual worlds over the past years has created new powerful ways for communications. Used intelligently, these communication mechanisms can propel people and businesses to new heights and also lows.

To be a better leader, or simply be better at something, it is worth looking at gaps and issues and how to address them. Most business problems I have seen have their root cause in poor communication directly followed by personal agendas versus working for the greater success of the company. The combination of our processing increasing amounts of information and publishing our opinions quickly and widely, when added to others' being able to alter them, redistribute them, and comment on them publicly, creates a dangerous environment where we can trip over yesterday's issues in an even bigger and amplified way in the virtual world.

How well you run your organization is directly related to your deep subject matter expertise, your vision, and your way of communication. The subject matter expertise and vision are on you. I will explore aspects of meshed online and offline communications to help raise awareness for you to be a better leader.

There are abstract communication channels, including appearance, speech, and writing. Each of these channels has an almost infinite variety of subtleties in terms of how we impact others, ranging from creating excitement, motivation, and satisfaction to possibly upsetting someone and everything in between.

Consider our gestures. Wizards of the Coast's ex-CEO Peter Adkison always gently smiled. No matter the specific situation, I can remember him only in a positive light. When I read his e-mails I interpreted them in the most respectful way because he is such a nice guy and can only have meant his words to be positive even though there can sometimes be ambiguity in online communication.

The below examples illustrate challenges we want to overcome in an increasingly dominant virtual world where fewer communication channels are available due to time zone differences, not being able to get everyone in the same room, and cultural aspects of whom we communicate with and how we communicate:

- At En Masse Entertainment, a U.S.-based triple A, MMORPG publisher, conducting international business is a core part of the day-to-day activities. The company is designed to bring top Asian MMOs to the western market. To do that, its key is excellent communication across multiple languages and time zones complemented by a strong leadership team with an excellent track record. Even though videoconferencing is used almost on a daily basis, it is not a replacement for in-person meetings. The company supports in-person meetings to increase its effectiveness knowing that it requires flying many of its employees a couple thousand miles to a different continent. The company also invests in full-time employee translators who are translating both spoken and written language even when the other party speaks the foreign language. The reason behind this is to avoid miscommunication. Even though we speak a second or third language, that does not guarantee we really understand those languages well enough to communicate accurately unless we are a professional translator.

- A human resources coordinator once told me that it is hard to see or feel people's energy online. She cannot look into their eyes, which is an important aspect of in-person communications. The personal connection is almost lost. As a result, she wants to overcommunicate without being repetitive, be super–detail oriented, thorough, and specific in her written e-mail communications to minimize miscommunication.
- A particular manager at T-Mobile had never seen some of his remote staff until they became friends on Facebook. He had to frequently remind himself that they were part of his team. The exclusive virtual world relationship made it hard for both the manager and his remote employees. In the back of his mind he was also never sure whether they were slacking off unless he was in frequent contact with them.
- A production assistant recently talked about the effort required to succeed in running a project that involved four different companies in four different locations and three different languages to accomplish one goal. It was tough.

When peeling back the onion and getting into the layers of organizational effectiveness, it is important to understand what motivates a workforce. Different people are motivated by different rewards. According to a brilliant study called "The Surprising Truth About What Motivates Us," published by RSA Animate on YouTube, people who perform mechanical work are most motivated by material rewards, whereas tasks that require even rudimentary cognitive skills are best performed when people understand the underlying purpose.

A good example is the Wikipedia project or any of the powerful

Open Source community software projects for which people do not get paid but still produce excellent results. How does this relate to our online and offline meshed communications? The better we understand the nature of what is involved to reach our objectives and the better we understand what motivates our workforce in relation to specific tasks, the more likely we are to succeed.

In the virtual world we have to be extra diligent to avoid misunderstandings because there are seldom quick private hints that would otherwise entice us to adjust our communications style to get the best out of a situation.

A good example is how to kick off projects. I am surrounded by great intelligent people. I thought it would suffice to assemble project documentation and requirements on a corporate wiki and ask engineers to get started working on the problem. I was wrong. The project review meeting turned into a kick-off meeting where it became clear that people needed to understand the purpose better to really excel at providing the best solution. Once we had time for a face-to-face discussion, things went impressively smoothly.

When talking with people in person, we have the luxury of using intonation, asking questions when we sense a disconnect, and quickly addressing gaps effectively. Did you ever come across two individuals who had a misunderstanding and reported their dissatisfaction to you as a manager in the organization? Both seeking a solution that they cannot achieve themselves? The only really effective way for long-term resolution is to get them in the same room and walk through what happened with both of them. This luxury may be absent in many virtual world situations.

When building your executive brand, do not underestimate the power of your appearance and the statements you make with it. Style goes a long way. Just perhaps reconsider entering a customer meeting with your Rolex and Armani suit when your products cost double that of your competition. You may create an impression that this is where the difference goes.

Consider leveraging video appearances on YouTube or other Internet or internal sites depending on the purpose of your message. This way you can compensate for the loss of the in-person touch. Companies like Microsoft have a long history of live streaming companywide and other meetings to their employees. Many managers also publish YouTube videos about technology deliverables.

Previously, the broader your role was, the more people knew you based on what you said and how you acted, versus the number of people you knew at the same level. In a meshed online and offline world, regardless of your role, just by merit of your information being on Flickr, Twitter, Facebook, LinkedIn, Google+, and similar services, the number of people who know you at a deeper level than you know them is likely greater for most of the readers of this book.

Do you remember impressive managers who knew everyone by name even in large organizations? Well, today in the virtual world everyone's name appears on an e-mail, and smart companies auto-attach employee photos for everyone who participates in the conversation. Attaching these photos is a great way of associating a face with a message. Now even you have a great chance to easily remember many coworker names. Try it.

For your written e-mail communications, think about everything you send as being public information no matter whether you act under nondisclosure or privacy statements. For exclusive virtual world communications, constantly remind yourself that there are resources you may be able to leverage even when you do not see them in person.

Consider your company culture and how to align it to get the highest organizational health index in a world that is full of opportunities to create communications problems even for the best of us. Balance your use of the online and offline meshed communications well. Unleash the potential of both worlds, and fuse them together through cohesion as part of your executive branding strategy. Do not rely on just one or the other.

Last but not least, people are your greatest assets, and not only the ones who directly report to you. Treat them like it. It will go a long way.

### REUVEN SUSSMAN, UNIVERSITY OF VICTORIA, CANADA

PhD in psychology. Has played drums for over 20 years mostly in funk bands and loves to busk on the street corner whenever possible. Hobbies: playing bicycle polo, solving puzzles, biking, hiking, and camping. Favorite saying: Be the change you want to see in the world.

I used to think that if I used my computer instead of going outside to enjoy the outdoors or meet people, I was a big loser. As a child growing up, I certainly developed my popularity more by joining sports teams and after-school activities than by staying in and playing Street Fighter 2 with my younger brother. That being said, things have changed dramatically since my early days, and I now believe that my "online persona" is capable of making me more popular rather than less.

I joined Facebook only to promote my band. After the experiences of my childhood, I had decided to try to cast off television and reduce my computer use as much as possible. I worked on my face-to-face communication skills and my appearance, and it was starting to pay off. To my surprise, people actually wanted to be around me, and I felt pretty good about it. So when my brother mentioned that I should join Facebook so I could get people to come see our band (by creating an "event"), I was understandably hesitant. Not only did I worry about putting my information on the Internet but I also didn't want to get sucked into a life of computer addiction because of a website my other friends were endearingly calling crackbook.

But I joined, and I really did get a lot more folks coming out to see us play. That's when I discovered the potential for this new media. What struck me almost immediately was that people I had met in person, who might have seemed rather boring in real life, often appeared to have crazy, extraverted, fun personas online. They were always posting pictures from parties or trips, commenting on other people's profiles, and starting or carrying on public conversations. What they may have lacked in face-to-face communication ability, they (perhaps unknowingly) made up for in online savvy.

I took this as a lesson in self-presentation and became sensitive to the image I was portraying online. I became so sensitive to it at one point, I decided to post a few pictures of myself on hotornot.com to see which one would get the best rating before using it as my profile picture—looking back, I think that was probably over the top.

I still use Facebook as a promotional tool, but now I realize the importance of also maintaining an online persona. If my promotional efforts are to remain effective, I must work at, and cultivate, my online persona to become "popular" in the new online world.

One important aspect of this is adding as many friends as possible to my online friends list. I learned that sometimes this can happen in strange ways. Once, after hearing about a couple with the exact same name (first and last) getting married because they met over Facebook, I decided to search my own name and see what happened.

Seeing as I had a rather unusual name (Reuven S), I was extremely surprised to find that there was another "Reuven S" in my city. Not only that, but after exchanging a few messages, I learned that we had actually met in elementary school! We became Facebook friends, and I still get a little surprised when reading news feed items about me that are actually about him.

Nowadays Facebook has become a vital part of my everyday existence. I joined, and I became addicted (as they said I would). However, I still use it less frequently than many of my friends, and I often think about the negative effects I might be experiencing from using it so much. My current graduate studies in environmental psychology have taught me about the negative effects of overstimulation and the restorative capacity of nature.

Humans have a limited capacity to take in information, and the constant bombardment of online advertising, videos, and pictures can be stressful. Conversely, our natural affiliation for the outdoors comes from our evolutionary past, and it has the potential to reduce stress and restore our cognitive resources. So I guess what I'm saying is that I no longer feel like a loser for spending so much time at my computer or on the Internet, but I do still feel that it's a very good idea to get outside as often as I can.

### RICK OWENS, CONVERGYS

Senior director at Cincinnati-based Convergys Corporation, where he leads the company's home agent program. Has over 20 years' experience in business transformation, process automation, workforce virtualization, and customer service. Has worked for the U.S. government, United Airlines, Qwest, TeleTech Holdings, and Alpine Access. Is married to his college sweetheart, Cathy Chapman. Three children: Matt (25), Troy (22), and Jenna (18). Hobbies: exercise, guitar, and photography. Favorite saying: "Control your own destiny or someone else will."—Jack Welch

In my youth, before I began my career in the early 1980s, I participated in the evolution of communications, when my family first got a touch-tone telephone and bought an answering machine. Yes, that was like the Stone Age, but it was impressive to see how much communications were changing, and it made me wonder where the changes might lead.

Fascinated with technology, I eventually pursued my undergraduate degree in software engineering. I'm a "punch card" guy. Years later, the first cellular phone I carried required a large, heavy bag over my shoulder and a wired handset. Later I carried "the brick": a modern "handheld" with a five-inch antenna that stuck out of it.

As a technology architect and engineer by trade and a corporate technical strategist, I have had a unique view of the communications evolution. For example, I was on the team that built the first online medical claims adjudication computer system for the U.S. Medicare program. Yes, my team carried the first terminals into hospitals, and I personally confronted "nurse Kratchet" at the door, who threatened my life because those darn computers would never enter the world of hospital care.

The government used to have semitrucks of paper medical claims that needed to be edited daily, which was done manually in large warehouses all over the country. Those first terminals in hospitals made entering that information much more efficient. We could communicate immediately that someone had just put a letter in her Social Security number . . . and to please correct it. You see, it's all about communication.

Today's generation is much more adept at handling a confusing, almost overwhelming flow of information and activity. Multitasking is no longer an exception that people must occasionally deal with. The current generation doesn't view multitasking as a new or temporary condition. Kids today with the highest GPAs are busy Tweeting, using Facebook, blogging, and texting almost nonstop.

When having a conversation with my kids, I used to stop

talking once in a while and ask a question because I didn't think they were listening to me. Surprisingly, almost 100 percent of the time, they could recite exactly what I had asked, then answer my question. Recently, looking at my phone bill, I saw that my 18-year-old had over 12,000 texts in one month. She also carries a 4+ GPA, plays guitar, and is an accomplished athlete.

For the past several years, I have held technology leadership positions in the call center industry. Today, I work from a home-based office, and I am responsible for managing a home agent program for a large outsourcer of agent-assisted services to multinational companies worldwide.

I require the leadership of my organization to work from their homes as well. We have evolved to working in St. Johns, Manitoba, Omaha, Winnipeg, Salt Lake City, Houston, Orlando, Denver, Cincinnati, and other cities. My teams cover all North American time zones, and we all flex our schedules and enjoy it very much.

My daily routine involves communication media using multiple PCs, my personal digital assistant (PDA), which is also a cellular phone, and a traditional landline telephone. I employ a continuous stream of e-mail, chat rooms and instant messaging, text messaging, virtual meeting technologies, and video.

For telephony, I use "unified communications," so I publish only one phone number, which I can have ring any phone numbers that I choose, simultaneously. Wherever I answer that call, the other phones stop ringing, and the caller doesn't know the call has been forwarded to a different phone. My voice mail is centralized, and each message is converted to text and sent to me via e-mail and text messages if the caller is someone I deem urgent or worthy of my immediate attention. In addition, any number I want blocked is done so instantly at my discretion.

Because of my exposure to the evolution of communication and information media, when I am meeting people or about to interview them for business, I normally investigate them through a web search, including blogs, other web or traditional publications, LinkedIn, and social networking sites like Facebook, Google+, and MySpace. I want to understand more about the people I'm about to interact with, to better grasp how they might communicate and what their paradigm could be. I find this jumpstarts the interaction and enables us to be most productive.

Over the years, I have introduced laypeople to these media. For example, I use Twitter to provide regular business status updates to my direct report managers or to the entire division, and I also use it to coordinate baseball practices for my children. I have held executive "chats" where all employees of my company could log into a chat room and get an update from me, then ask questions.

I have conducted interviews using videoconferencing from a hotel room 5,000 miles from the candidates I needed to speak to. For videoconferencing services, I routinely use Skype and FaceTime, primarily with my family, including my 80-year-old in-laws who have learned to appreciate these technologies.

I take a camera, write my own copy, and produce a four-minute video welcoming new employees. I tell them about the company, about the project they'll be working on, and about my expectations in a motivating way. We can monitor which employees click on and watch and for how long or if they click off before it finishes. I can ask them about it: "Was it boring? Not helpful?" While being helpful to them, they also understand they are being monitored. Even if I don't create a video, when I send an e-mail, I have my photo in the signature so people can see the person they are talking to. It personalizes it a little.

Daily, I use systems like Microsoft Live, GoToMeeting, and WebEx to share presentations and other applications or materials with audiences around the world on topics relating to business, technology, and other matters.

Becoming ever more popular is video messaging. I have begun taping messages for new-hire employees, and the messages have become part of the hiring process to let everyone hear from me personally—a welcome message and advocacy for the need for them to deliver top quality customer service even though they might never meet someone from our company face-to-face.

Whenever I travel to a city, I look up one of our home agents and stop by for a visit. Most times, I'm the first person they have met from our company. They typically appreciate the opportunity to work flexible schedules around their lives and the fact that they do not need to buy a wardrobe or commute to an office.

I have begun using videoconferencing over the web with my staff as well to continue trying new, advancing communication methods. I've found it less productive for impromptu meetings. Some folks don't like suddenly having to be presentable. (We have a new term—not video ready (NVR)—for those times you just don't want to be seen yet.) My goal is to keep growing my arsenal of tools for interaction in a "constantly shrinking world."

My daughter recently left home to attend the University of Georgia, which is 1,471 GPS-derived miles from my home, to be exact. She is adept with many forms of communication. Our family uses text, e-mail, and videoconferencing to stay involved in her life. We employ these tools from PCs and PDAs. For example, we can quickly connect our PC to a big screen TV and conduct high-definition video calls in which she can take us on spontaneous tours of her dorm and campus. When she turns an ankle playing soccer, we can see the swelling and watch her treatments. When her roommates and she get dressed up, we can meet the companions. We can see a storm as it is happening in the area. And family meals with my wife and sons can still somewhat involve our daughter although she is two time zones away.

I have digressed. As CEOs and as leaders, we must demonstrate the practice of continual learning. The speed of business evolution requires moving data and information quickly. The CEO sets the pace and momentum of the organization, and the foundation of that structure is communication.

To compete, we must take advantage of every tool available to us—the concept of a shrinking world is real. We now collaborate and compete globally whether we like it or not. The key is to not let this change intimidate us.

I like to think of it this way: exercise makes one stronger. Make it a habit to bring new communication into your everyday life, to practice. Then you can take advantage of these tools in the business world. If you just relax, you'll find it's fun and really not that difficult, despite the new vocabulary (Google, tweet, blog, IM, and so on).

Many people avoid innovation and miss out on wonderful opportunities to broaden their capabilities. I have colleagues and friends who won't e-mail, blog, tweet, IM, or text. I can only say to them: enjoy the sidelines. The game will continue without you.

### SUSAN SCHELL, BUSINESS ACUMEN, LLC

President. On faculty at Colorado State University. Business experience spans 40 years and has included manufacturing, service, retail, healthcare, energy, banking, education, and finance. Two adult children: Tracy and Damon. Four grandchildren: Kasandra, Kaidon, Kiera, and Kendal. Hobbies: writing, travel, antique collecting, interior design, and crafts. Favorite saying: If two people in a room agree on everything, one of them is unnecessary.

I worked as a top-level executive in a high-technology company for 18 years. The equipment that we invented was used in the semiconductor manufacturing industry. We were enabling chip technology to be used to produce smaller, denser, cheaper, and more reliable equipment.

What a wonderful industry this was to be in during the booming years of technological breakthroughs and surprising new scientific advances. We were not only helping the evolution of technology but we were also using it in creative and facilitating ways. Now, as a professional business consultant and investment banker, I continue to use the ever-improving technology as a key part of business practices.

One client was emotionally ready to sell his business. However, with a recent recession and loss of profitability, the probability of a good sale price was very low. To guide him toward a better bottom line, I became the "Virtual CEO" for one year until the sale was accomplished. I worked remotely via computer on problem solving, hiring, evaluating critical metrics, improving quality, recommending ways to enhance profitability, and a host of other projects. I was available virtually for any crisis including a surprise Occupational Safety and Health Administration (OSHA) audit, which I discreetly coached them through as it was occurring with the help of cell phone earpieces and text messaging. In today's environment and with multiple locations for many businesses, remote monitoring and virtual management are essential and can be extremely effective.

Business sale transactions require a great deal of information to be gathered during a process called "due diligence." The process can involve having potential buyers pour over copious amounts of information at a client's location. Several years ago, we converted to a "virtual data room" that allowed hard copies of information to be scanned into the computer and presented online to the buyers and their representatives. It changed the process from a site-centered, paper-intensive one to an encrypted, password-protected, highly monitored, low-cost solution.

Now the information can be viewed from any location in the

world, at any time of the day or night. What a fabulous way to simplify the most difficult process in the sale of a company while increasing the geographic reach of the business and allowing access to be strictly controlled.

A potential client invited me to his business for a discussion. He was professional and well spoken. His desire was to divest of his company that he had built for over 30 years. I was interested in helping, but I had a strange gut feeling that there was something suspicious about him. When he left the room for a few minutes to get some paperwork, I used my iPad and looked him up on CoCourts.com, a Colorado website and one of many websites that allows you to see public records. I was able to find that he had a long and frightening history of legal issues including acting as a defendant 45 times, almost always for nonpayment of debts.

By the time he came back into the room, I was able to decline the engagement and avert a potentially difficult situation down the road. Quick data references are available to all of us. Using them for critical business information may keep you out of court.

In a teaching role at Colorado State University, I am part of a distance-learning MBA program that reaches students in 30 countries. Through streaming video and DVD distribution, the courses are delivered to 1,200 students worldwide. Although I see only the 30 students who are seated in the actual classroom, I have been touched by students all over the world.

On one occasion, a student phoned me to say that I had just saved his company because of the nature of the course material we were covering. It was extremely gratifying to know that my information could be used simultaneously by hundreds of remote students in as many companies, impacting the world.

What used to be a brick-and-mortar institution is now delivered around the world to people in the military, business, government, and nonprofits in the privacy of their locations. Similarly, businesses create their own internal universities for their employees and economically provide virtual training and employee development worldwide.

I use thousands of websites for business. I search for potential employees, solicit clients, check references, learn about new technology, deliver training, and talk on Skype with remote colleagues. We use our own website to deliver critical information, to house an "impact video" about our business, and we are just beginning the process of incorporating CR [customer relationship] technology to earmark key information to potential clients.

In 1980, I spent 90 percent of my time walking around the business and creating written reports. Today, I spend 90 percent of my time walking around a virtual world and creating enormous value.

### HEIDI A. OLINGER, PRETTY BRAINY

Chief executive officer. Fashion designer, writer, and adjunct professor of journalism. Hobbies: Ashtanga yoga, hiking, birdwatching with partner, CEO Jim Striggow. Favorite saying: "If you must do a thing, do it graciously."—Alice B. Toklas

I suspect that online dating and doing business online share a few sins. Online or off, I have never joined a dating service, but it is common sense that people in the dating and business worlds share the idea that they will put their best selves forward.

I say idea because the ground between intention and result can be a long, deserted highway. Personal photos are a prime online telltale: I could name names of the contacts in my LinkedIn account whose photos look nothing like the people who sit across from me over coffee. I would swear in court that one contact stole and uploaded someone else's image.

The word *expert* is another telltale sign, and my story hinges on the misuse of *expert*, *expertise*, and *specialist*.

We may experience the virtual world as anonymous and impersonal, but flesh-and-blood, heart-pumping human beings are behind what we see online. We owe it to ourselves to ask, "Who are these people?" We equally are accountable for answering, "Who am I?"

There is a proliferation of "experts" in online blogging when it comes to topics like "Five Ways to Boost Sales." When any expert is introduced to us as the person who will "fix" our website, our lie-detector sensors need to be on. "Three Moves for Eliminating Backache" came through my Droid one night after working too long at the computer. This was just what I needed. But though the source was a company I like, the moves were neither new nor healing, and the real message was, "Buy our exercise ball."

Don't lie. This is one of the first lessons adults and the Church teach us when we are children. It is also the biggest online sin some businesspeople commit. Tell the truth. Don't misrepresent.

To the job applicant who looks good on paper, I like to say, "What will we find out about you in three months that we won't see today?" Now I apply this guideline to vendors who "specialize" or are "expert" in new media.

The lesson I learned is this: the insight for figuring out how my company can use new media to help make customers' lives better rests on me, the CEO. No one is going to care about my customers' experiences as much as I do.

Knowing how to lead online is a matter of hands-on experience. Forget about dropping all of the techno-assignments on the youngest, geekiest members of the team. Their natural inclination for technology is a myth. *CEO* now means *chief experience officer*, and the learning curve can be quick.

Use the media your customers are using. Use your competitors' websites. If your customers are shopping online, you shop online. If they are posting Facebook updates from their smart phones, you post Facebook updates from your smart phone. Experience what they experience. Sign up for online newsletters. Sign up for text messages to your phone. Pay attention to your gut reaction as a user and recipient. When my phone rang on a Saturday at 7 a.m. to deliver a text message that my oil needed to be changed, I changed garages.

A conversation I had with a former marketing assistant went like this:

Me: What are you doing?
She: E-mail.
Me: Yeah, but what are you working on?
She: E-mail. I'm reading my e-mail.
Me: Look at me.
She: What?
Me: E-mail isn't a real thing. The upcoming event is a real thing. Getting the press to the event definitely is real. But e-mail is just a tool. When you leave here for a different job, are you going to list on your résumé, "Read e-mail"?

I love the woman, but until that conversation she thought e-mail was the means and the end. E-mail connects people. The same goes for Twitter, Facebook, and YouTube. Use them if your customers use them. At the same time, do not expect social media to affect the bottom line. After a string of bad "marriages" to bad web developers who promised the sky, I hammered out a media plan based on the following. Figure out:

- Where customers are online
- What content attracts them

- What devices they are using to get there
- How they behave once they arrive

In Texas there is an old saying about wannabes: "Big Hat, No Cows." It's one thing if the guy next door lies about his spread. It is another if a web developer lies about his capabilities.

No matter how entrepreneurial you and I may be, when it comes to the company website, we are held hostage by at least two elements:

1. Not fully knowing how to code a functional website
2. The lag time between when a developer is given a project and when he or she gets it done

In the fourth quarter of 2010, I revamped my company sales model. E-commerce became a cornerstone. I had studied the gold standard of e-commerce sites, and I took my knowledge to the principal of our latest web development company. He had been updating me on a new software feature that his coder had just that afternoon installed on our site. The coder quietly worked in his cubicle. He was wearing his Star Wars t-shirt. He once had uploaded Star Wars images to our website in a demonstration. I do not recall ever hearing him speak.

Eager to show off the progress, the principal and I peered into the monitor of his laptop. He refreshed the page, and all of our product photos disappeared. A wide gap stretched from the top of the page. The coder had made the change before lunch. The time was 4:30 p.m. I fired the developer.

It was then that I realized I had failed to lead these people in seeing the vision of serving visitors. The coder, a nice boy, did not understand the women on the front end of the site. They make demands of their online experience, and we have seconds to deliver. The coder saw code and the cool things it could do. He had no concept of my customer.

I needed to marry the front-end vision to the back-end vision, and I needed a developer with the integrity and work ethic to hold both. I also needed to get elbow deep in the back end of a site so I could communicate with the next developer.

I was in for another digital divorce, but now I understood what I had to do to make the next relationship work. I needed firsthand understanding of the developer's tools and how to use them to serve customers and communicate our brand.

Our current designer-developer stands apart from the crowd. Her attitude is upbeat. Her outlook is about service. Before beginning the makeover of our website, she had no experience in the e-commerce software I had chosen. She had minimal experience in the blog software we had been using for two years. But she trained herself on her time at her own expense. She has an open mind. She works fast.

She created design mock-ups of every idea that came out of my head. When I saw that her preferred mode of communication was e-mail, I used e-mail to keep momentum high. I have learned to be explicit in my requests and instructions. I write brief sentences. I number every point.

Any jerk can have a title and a big salary. But leaders lead by being worthy of leading. For six months in 2010, veteran journalist Jill Abramson stepped back from her role as the managing editor of the *New York Times*. Her purpose? To learn firsthand how to incorporate what she knew, print journalism, with what she had to learn, online journalism. In September 2011 she became the first woman in the paper's history to lead, being named its executive editor.

Lead, but competently lead. Learn how your customers and your tech team each experience the digital world. This is a fresh road for leadership. And that is the truth.

## KARLA R. PETERS-VAN HAVEL, INSTITUTE FOR MANAGEMENT STUDIES (IMS)

Vice president. Former companies: Citadel Communications and Jackson Radio, where she was a news director and talk-show host. Teaches drama, art, public speaking, leadership, and communication skills to gifted teenagers. Likes hot air ballooning, kayaking, hiking volcanoes, traveling, and building things. Children: Ashley, Jason, Courtney, and AFS daughter from Japan, Hiromi. Hobbies: PhD work, research on brain dynamics. Favorite saying: Nothing will ever be attempted if all possible objections must first be overcome.

I have seen the stereotypes and expectations of online audiences, and they are not always accurate. All speakers, especially those in leadership positions, must know their audience. But what if you have never met your audience?

In many corporations, technology has replaced the corporate communications person, leaving a CEO or an executive naked to an unknown audience. In other organizations the corporate communications person is on scene, but only to anticipate questions and prepare a C-suite officer for upcoming events such as an earnings call. Blogs, e-mails, social networks, tweets, Second Life presentations, weblogs, or other social collaboration tools are often recorded and open to global interpretation, and more often than not, they are the true unadulterated word of a CEO or top executive. So when you don't know anything about your audience, how do you present to that audience?

Since there is no denying the influx of technology and the greater dependence our society has on it, there is an urgent need for the world of business to understand how to best communicate with this new breed of "plugged-in" businesspeople. While all kinds of research is being done on this topic in regards to the long-term effects of technology on the brain, it is hard to conclusively give a cause and effect for the changes in oxygen in the blood to specific areas in the brain. This is what functional magnetic resonance imaging (fMRI) actually measures.

What the fMRI can show is that some neural networks are stronger due to more use while other areas may be weaker due to less use. This is not necessarily a negative thing. However, not all recipients of an organization's message are digital natives or even digital immigrants. Some are in digital denial, but executives have to be prepared so that those in digital denial also get their message. Cerebrodiversity must be accounted for because synaptic connections vary depending on experiences.

When the audience is diverse, with different levels of technological and business knowledge, with brains that may interpret a message differently than the sender intended it, how do CEOs or executives communicate? The answer is to assume nothing and plan for everything. That means communicating in the technological world while continuing to communicate in the nondigital world for those that prefer hard copy. It also means addressing staccato ways of thought by keeping things exciting, short, and bulleted, while remaining authentic. And it means storytelling while sharing.

Part of being an effective CEO is being an effective communicator regardless of the audience or medium. For example, a communication gone wrong occurs at a medium-sized international company I will call XYZ. The CEO of XYZ decides to be the one to announce an updated system to the current conferencing format the company was using to coordinate with its transcontinental teams. It is an opportunity to roll out a new format and motivate and re-engage stakeholders (employees, customers, board members, and investors). The announcement is done in a way the CEO is most familiar with, via e-mail.

After the normal welcomes and kind biddings, the CEO jumps into his message:

"We have upgraded our antiquated screen-shot-only remote

conferencing capabilities to a new system called Skype. This is a format that offers group videoconferencing along with the ability to instant message during a call to an individual or the group as a whole without interrupting the conference. The use of this software application by all within XYZ will offer a cohesive brand internally and externally. An online training session will be offered on Monday and Tuesday for our friends who still prefer a typewriter to a computer. The new system is now accessible, and the old software will no longer be available for your use after the first of the month."

The presentation was six paragraphs long with detail about the training times and places and how cutting edge this new videoconferencing will make XYZ.

Do you see the faux pas? One error is in the method of communication and judging that all stakeholders will receive, use, and respect a letter from the CEO in e-mail format. Another is the segregation by age and the assumption that the elder generation, that once perhaps used a typewriter, is less knowledgeable about videoconferencing systems. Additionally there is an assumption that the younger audience members do not need training. And the CEO is assuming that the Skype format is an enormous upgrade that will bring the company closer together. However, many technologically savvy personnel of diverse ages and experiences are familiar with even newer systems and perhaps feel Skype is antiquated by today's standards, thus not cutting edge at all. The challenge is that this e-mail will be recorded in history, and it will frame future discussions about technology and age bias in the workplace.

One potential solution to addressing a diverse audience with which you are unfamiliar is to vary the media used to correspond. Possible outlets could be a combination of a newsletter, bulletin board, central broadcast, staff meeting, corporate blog such as Socialcast, along with an e-mail and a videoconference. It is also important to avoid jargon but to still explain why the change. For instance, a leader could report "We have chosen this particular system because . . ." and then explain that the upgrade to live video from screen shots and audio is supportable and used industrywide for greater accessibility by all, rather than focusing on it as "cutting edge."

Finally, no references to age or technical ability need be included. A much less controversial lead-in to the training would be to explain that although many employees may already be familiar with Skype and do not need training, for those that are not, or would like a refresher, training is available.

So when you don't know anything about your audience and it is up to you to present as the leader of an organization, it is better to assume nothing, present in a manner fitting diversity, use multiple forms of communication, and invite questions. By doing this we overcome synaptic connection diversity. Whether one is a digital native, digital immigrant, or is in digital denial, we can open the communication channels and avoid the communication issue so many of us face as best described in the statement by Robert McClosky: "I know that you believe you understand what you think I said, but I'm not sure you realize that what you heard is not what I meant."

**MARK CHAMBERS, QSPIKE**

Chief executive officer. Former companies: Tech-Agent, Knowledge-Design, and TechStart. Four daughters who all love to go big game hunting. Hobbies: photography, reading, and eating good food. Favorite saying: Plan for the rule, not the exception.

I was faced with this challenge when I posted my first blog entry: I was staring at an empty screen wondering what I was going to write about. What would be interesting that hadn't already been said a thousand times over, by people much more qualified to speak than me? And yet I wanted to write! I wanted to have a voice! That first post was like countless other first posts: "A Company Is Born."

When I look back at that and a few following it, I cringe. Granted, I was new at it, and with experience, things improve, but at the time I had not found my "sea legs" in writing. It even felt a little like being seasick when approaching a new post. But over time, it got easier. Now I am no expert, but I will say—if you want to get better at writing . . . Write!

Over time you will find a voice begin to emerge. You begin to see patterns of topics that just seem to "feel right." When you reach that, embrace it and don't let go! Cultivate it. Talk with people about it. Learn all you can about it, and internalize it so that when someone asks you on the street, you can have a deep conversation about it.

That is why people will want to read what you have to say about a subject—even if it has been written about by 100 other people: because you are knowledgeable and you have passion! That passion comes through the page (or screen) and grips the readers. They are feeding off of that energy and feel better for it.

So find your social voice and write! Don't give up! People are interested and need to hear what you have to say. And don't forget to have some Dramamine on hand.

## CHRISTOPHER SEEGERS, GRACE / MAYER INSURANCE AGENCY

Account executive. Grew up in Chichuhua, Mexico. Spends weekends on family ranch in southern Colorado building fences, assisting in hay and cattle production, and researching ways to make small production agriculture sustainable in today's economic climate. Hobbies: anything that makes him "intellectually uncomfortable," composing and playing music, and any sport with a board. Favorite saying: It is not what you know but whom you surround yourself with.

I was fresh out of graduate school and had just landed a dream job at a large insurance brokerage firm. I was ecstatic, and the earning possibilities seemed limitless. The position I had taken was as an account executive, which is a dressed up way of saying "salesperson." My plan was to receive company training in the Midwest at the corporate headquarters and then return to my home state to grow the company's book of business in that region.

Time flew, as it does, and soon enough I was itching to build a book of business and prove myself to my bosses back at the corporate office. I am an astute individual, and so I had taken it upon myself to learn as much about being a successful salesperson as possible during my training. I had picked up on many different sales techniques including hard sells, soft sells, wedging, cold calling, imitation, and countless other methods that I took into my arsenal as I moved into the marketplace. My company had also equipped me with the latest software and hardware, as they were firm believers in using "gadgets" in the sales process.

Being new to the business, I began to research my industry, and I decided that I would search out the hundred largest clients in each sector and target them as my first prospects. This strategy was incredibly ambitious, and my bosses warned against it and advised me to start small and work my way up the prospect food chain. I disregarded their advice, however, as I figured if I was going to be in this business, I wanted to be the best and only pursue the types of accounts that would really challenge me.

The chase began shortly after, and what a wild ride it was! I leveraged all of my training and hit those prospects with e-mails, cold calls, drip marketing, and links to videos and news articles, and I was even shameless enough to try to message executives on LinkedIn. I was tireless in my pursuit, and I kept at it for months before I came to a realization: what I was doing was absolutely not working. But how could this be? I had taken my comprehensive virtual business training from business school and combined it with the latest and greatest sales techniques into a strategy that on paper should have been flawless, and yet I was failing.

Failing can be a great thing as it can often lead to introspection, and so I looked inward. I asked myself, why was I failing and what could I do differently? After days of struggling, I realized it came down to the way that I was treating the people I interacted with. I was treating people as business prospects instead of living, breathing human beings. I was hammering them with impersonal communication, and I realized that I was essentially treating them as machines.

I had become so entangled in our virtual society that I had forgotten my agricultural roots where you know your neighbor, and the people that you do business with are the people that you know and trust to look out for your best interests. I decided to try a new sales strategy based on one basic principle: *get to know each and every prospect face-to-face.*

I hit the road and began to drive to each prospect's office with a very simple intro: "I know you are busy so I won't take much of your time, but I wanted to stop by and introduce myself to you face-to-face and let you know that I believe we have some products and services that would be worth our setting up a formal appointment to go over."

I received a variety of reactions, but all but one (an owner who was a notorious old curmudgeon) were positive. Many of the executives even thanked me for taking the time to swing by in person, and they often invited me into their offices to converse further. These men and women often opened up and explained to me that they had never had someone from the insurance industry stop in to meet them personally, and they were exhausted by the barrage of e-mails and telephone calls from salespeople trying to court them.

My strategy was so simple it was stupid, and yet it worked over and over again. My sales figures skyrocketed, and soon other salespeople were coming to me to ask how I was doing so well. I explained to them my simple plan, and they often shook their heads and gave me reasons why it wouldn't work for them, and then they returned to their e-mail campaigns.

The business world is evolving and the virtual tools at our disposal are innumerable and often very powerful, but we often forget one thing: at the other end of those virtual tools is another human being who deserves respect, and nothing is more powerful than a handshake and a few minutes of face time.

### JOEY UNGERER, FINE TUNE FEATURES

Founder. Graphic designer for Hard Rock Hotel and Casino in Las Vegas. Worked on the film crew of The Bachelor. Was voted "Best Heart" in high school. Hobbies: enjoys illustrating, snowboarding, and photography. Favorite saying: The harder I try, the luckier I get.

Throughout the last 10 years of my life, computers (and the Internet more specifically) have become a more and more necessary means of communication. I remember being told in my very first college class (2002) that I had the option to find my homework in my e-mail's inbox. I remember thinking, "Well, it's not required. I'm not getting an e-mail address." By the following year, it was required. But that didn't matter because I had already submitted, and I had registered for an e-mail account . . . along with this new thing called a "Facebook" Profile.

Seemingly overnight, online communication went from nuisance to necessary. By 2004, I was submitting homework to teachers via e-mail, "Due by midnight." I also had a job at the college newspaper. I wrote and illustrated a daily cartoon strip that was submitted each day at 5 p.m. via e-mail.

Since graduating from college, I have realized that online

communication may be convenient, but it has also created a void in personal interaction. The ease of writing a sincere-sounding e-mail seems impersonal. This is why I like to approach prospective new employers in person. This way, I can shake their hand, and they are more likely to remember my face. But I was too late. By the time I had graduated college, e-mail was such a preferred method of communication that I didn't have the option to provide a personal touch anymore.

One day, I printed up my résumé on the best résumé paper I could find. It had a good "bone" color and the perfect tooth (texture) for pensive fingers. I went into a marketing agency with the intent of meeting whoever was available. I simply walked in the front door and cheerfully introduced myself to the receptionist. Giving me the "limo noodle" handshake, she gazed back at me with a furrowed brow and mouth half-open as if someone had just said "Checkmate" on his first move in a game of chess.

She clearly wasn't going to introduce herself back to me, so I broke the silence with, "I have admired the portfolio of advertising work that comes out of this agency. I just thought I'd drop by and see if I can shake a few hands and meet a few people."

With a sigh, she said in a monotone voice, "If you are looking for a job, that's done online. Send your résumé to info@ xcompany.com."

I knew how this conversation was going to go, but I put on my naïve face and said, "Oh, I just wanted to meet some people and get to know a few names."

She flashed a quick sarcastic smile and said, "Your best bet is e-mail."

Looking past her desk, I noticed several office doors that were open. Our conversation had caught the attention of a couple of computer slaves, who I can only assume were hopeful of contact from "the outside world." When my eyes met those of a man behind a desk labeled "creative director," the man quickly corrected his eavesdropping posture and went back to typing. Surprising only to me, I left the office, satisfied that I would not be working there.

With hundreds of job seekers applying online to every job posting that pops up, it's no wonder that companies don't think twice about ignoring most of the applicants. It has been four years since I graduated from college. Online and mobile phone communications have been a daily staple in my routine.

I e-mailed Debra about an opportunity that was presented to me back in January of 2011. I had broken up with my fiancé and was managing a portrait studio. A family friend was offering me a job in the reality TV business. Without hesitation, Debra advised me to take the leap. I did, and here is what has happened:

In February, I moved out to California bringing my new smart phone and only the possessions that would fit in my Pontiac Grand Am. I slept on a friend's couch, and I worked 12-hour days for the first month. I then found an apartment and continued working for various TV shows. By the third month, I had worked for *The Bachelor, The Bachelorette, Bachelor Pad, Tia & Tamera,* and *Bar Rescue.*

Through this very mobile time in my life, my smart phone kept me connected to the world. Having never visited LA before, the maps on my phone helped me to navigate the hairy traffic. I was also able to receive e-mails and text messages from employers regarding instructions for my job. There were even a couple times when I was chosen for a certain task because I had a smart phone. I recall one day when my manager (on *The Bachelor* TV show) shouted, "We have to get the Bachelor to the airport! Who has a smart phone that can take him there?" Being the only one with a smart phone, I got the job. Being only my second day on an internationally acclaimed TV show, this opportunity was thrilling to say the least.

While working on the show *Bar Rescue,* a producer noticed

my graphic design talents and appointed me "head of the graphic design department." The show visits bars around the United States that are struggling and failing. The host of our show remodels the buildings and business structure of each bar. I was responsible for designing the logos, billboards, signs, and clothing for each bar that we visited. With *Bar Rescue* on my résumé, I continued looking for graphic design work outside of California. I updated my personal portfolio website. I had had a Twitter account for a couple years, but I never really bothered to tweet. About one month ago, I decided to spend an entire day tweeting about my website and about thoughts on graphic design.

Three days and 60 tweets later, I had 85 new followers, and two e-mails in my inbox from people who wanted graphic design work done for them (potentially worth about $1,000 of income). Over the past month, I have tweeted about three times per day, and traffic to my website has more than quadrupled! I have also had a greater response to job applications. I interviewed for a job as a graphic designer for the Hard Rock Casino in Las Vegas! This face-to-face interview was held in California.

The following day after the interview (while I was sitting in the audience of *The Price Is Right!!*), the casino e-mailed to request an over-the-phone interview with me. I was excited about this opportunity as it's a huge job within my career field. I had the conference call, held between three people all located in different places in the country, and it ended with my getting the job! *Sigh—sweet, sweet technology.

### RICK AMBROSE, LOCKHEED MARTIN'S INFORMATION SYSTEMS AND GLOBAL SOLUTIONS-NATIONAL (IS&GS-NATIONAL)

President, IS&GS-National, a company that has just under 7,000 employees that deliver highly advanced systems and services to the

U.S. intelligence community and international customers. Hobbies: golf and travel. Three children. Married 31 years. Believes honesty, trust, and integrity are the underlying foundational components of successful relationships between senior management and its employees. Believes these elements become even more critical when leading a geographically diversified workforce.

Along with many other corporations and corporate stakeholders, Lockheed Martin is embracing new social media capabilities—but the corporate world is not alone in this transformation. Even teachers are changing the way they teach, and family members are adjusting how they communicate with each other as a result of the "social media phenomenon."

At Lockheed Martin, our younger workers have grown up with Google, Facebook, and Twitter. They are used to obtaining information as soon as the desire to do so crosses their mind. Why then, should a corporation like ours have a communication model that results in a slow trickle-down of information, open to interpretation and delay? Why shouldn't we provide information to our employees right away, straight from the source, through multiple, interactive channels—something that has become the norm in every other aspect of life?

But is this really what employees prefer? Do young workers want face time, or do they want online communication? I think they want both—after all, they receive both in their everyday lives. So I have tried to provide my employees face time, which is often seen as productive, meaningful, and somewhat comforting in times of economic strain, but also online options, to provide the speed and availability that so many of us have become used to.

In the past, we communicated with employees in a way that saturated them with one-way transmission of data. Using this style of communication, it's very difficult for them to discern important communications from routine communications, let alone keep things timely and accurate. As a result, employees may begin to shut out the communication all together because it takes too much effort to decipher the meaning.

At IS&GS-National, we have been trying to give our employees two-way communication options that exist both virtually and in person. The first six months we pursued this shift, we gained some lessons learned when it comes to leading in a virtual world.

We have created an integrated communications approach that includes a variety of face-to-face and online channels. These channels include live webcasts, broadcast teleconferences, newsletters, microblogs, blogs, town halls, and skip-level meetings, where a cross-section of employees meet with senior leadership over lunch.

The town halls and skip-level meetings provide the face-to-face time that employees need. The online communication technology allows us to reach our dispersed workforce, unlimited by business area, geography, and time constraints. However, certain other constraints exist with online communications such as export control regulations when communicating with a global audience.

We quickly learned our employee base was extremely appreciative of the honest nature of these types of communications—whether face-to-face or online. Even though at times they may disagree with the perspective in the message, the honest, frank nature of the communication is appreciated, as it is seen as respectful.

The following are the types of communication channels we have implemented at Lockheed Martin's IS&GS-National division.

### BROADCASTS

Broadcasts are aired in two primary ways: video feeds (online shows transmitted live with the ability to ask questions and give answers in real time) and audio only (one-way live teleconferences). The intent of broadcasts is to reach a large audience of employees across multiple geographic sites, in a timely manner with a consistent message. The primary advantage of this type of communication is location, location, location! Our employees work all over the world. These broadcast sessions give them the ability to see and hear us, ask questions right away, all the while never leaving their desk. If the employees aren't available to join the session live, they also have the ability to replay prior events online.

### MICROBLOGS

This channel is great for fast, simple communication like giving a "shout-out" or a pat on the back. Everyone likes to be recognized, so this kind of informal, positive reinforcement receives a lot of positive response. Our internal version of microblogging is similar to Twitter. Employees can share everything from "leftover lunch in conference room A" to conversations between multiple people, to self-promotion, to articles they've read and have found useful.

There are some challenges associated with communicating via microblogs. One challenge is the intimidation felt by some employees when it comes to responding to senior executives. Another is the public nature of posts where everyone can see what you've written and who you are. Microblogs provide very little anonymity.

### BLOGS

In order to facilitate a more in-depth, informative conversation, we decided to launch a blog. This medium allowed us to address relevant issues facing our business and employees. Most posts are centralized around "rumors" and controversial topics that our employee base wants to hear about. Also, in many cases, posts are developed based on high interest employee questions that have been raised in town halls and skip-level meetings. These issues cover relevant topics such as performance management and career development. Some posts describe case studies of successful programs. Some are written by guest bloggers.

We learned from employee feedback that managers were using the blog to initiate open discussions with their teams. In addition, employees are taking the initiative to use the blog as a forum for open discussion among themselves.

I think part of the reason the blog has been successful is because we are open and transparent with our employees. We do not hide behind any corporate boundaries, and we don't make announcements. We share stories. The blog provides pertinent information we know our employees want to hear more about, resources, and "news you can use." Every entry is "scannable" and short, it's written in a conversational tone, and we share our honest opinions while at the same time welcoming criticism.

### TOWN HALL MEETINGS

We put a plan in place to accomplish 10 town hall sessions in six months. The goal of these town halls is to be unconventional and to not follow the standard corporate flow-down of information informally known as "death by PowerPoint" (80 percent of time allocated to slides with only 20 percent left for questions and answers).

With these town halls, we want to spark candid conversations with our employees and talk about their underlying concerns and challenges. Not only does this channel of communication provide face-to-face interaction for employees but it also gives me and the rest of our leaders knowledge we couldn't have gained anywhere else. I always come away understanding what is working and what is not working and with a clear focus on what issues we should address next.

### SKIP-LEVELS

We also have another form of employee sessions called "skip-levels." They are held in an informal matter, often times over breakfast or lunch. The meal seems to create a comforting environment. We also try to maintain an intimate setting by having groups of fewer than 20 employees. In most situations, these sessions provide the greatest source of candor and explanation of deep issues that are affecting employees. It is from these intimate gatherings that we often gather topics to address through our online communication channels.

### LEADERSHIP

We have been very consistent in our direction to executive and senior leaders to create and maintain an environment of trust and respect. Dick Brown (former chair and CEO of Electronic Data Systems) was famous for noting, "People are not afraid of change. They fear the unknown." We need to ensure that as an organization, we do a better job making the unknown known. The best way I know how to do that is by keeping the channels of communication open.

### FEEDBACK

Whereas most corporations are lucky to reach a 10 percent employee engagement rate with their communication efforts, we have been pleasantly surprised with our measurements. In just four months, my blog Rick's Roundtable has been visited by nearly 50 percent of our employees. The number of visitors continues to climb, and our goal is to reach 100 percent of employees by the end of the year. Among the employees who have visited my blog, feedback has been positive. For example, in an e-mail to her 18 employees, a manager wrote, "Please take a few minutes to read the blog at the link below. It is some professional advice we can all use. I think he stated it very well."

We've also stayed on track for reaching our targeted number of employees at town halls. We obtained feedback specifically about the town halls by placing an anonymous, hard copy survey along with a Lockheed Martin pen on employees' chairs. This gave attendees the incentive to fill out the survey right then and there. This was great because not only did we get instant feedback—in some cases, we took feedback from a morning session and made improvements to the afternoon session— but we saw a very strong response rate. One employee stated, "Grateful to see they're not talking at us—enjoyed the two-way dialogue." Another said, "I will share this with my employees at our staff meeting this afternoon."

The surveys were a half-page, with five quantitative questions on the front that asked employees to rate a few key items: Did you learn more about strategy? Were we candid and honest? Did we cover the topics you want to hear about? Did you learn something you can take action on? Will you attend the next town hall? On the back, we asked three qualitative questions: What did you like most? What were your two biggest takeaways? How would you improve future sessions? We found that asking these questions up front often got employees in a more productive mindset. They were more focused on strategy, more willing to speak up, and more focused on things they could take back to their desks.

### CRITICAL SUCCESS FACTORS

This process has taught us much about what employees appreciate when receiving communication from upper management. We are all busier than ever, so understanding what drives employees to take the time to read and participate is crucial to success.

First, "news you can use": Employees must understand how the communication helps them perform their job better or makes their job easier. They need to feel like there will be tangible results and real-life gains. The other side of "news you can use" is how employees come away feeling about the communication. If they feel inspired or educated after participating, that can be just as useful.

Second, messages must be frank, honest, edgy, and respectful. Employees don't want to be talked "at" or lectured to, and they will sniff out and reject anything they receive as corporate "spin." This can be a little uncomfortable at first, but the return on investment is worth it. Employees don't pay attention to announcements—they listen to stories. We're up front about communicating setbacks, but we never criticize the teams.

Third, leaders and managers are a huge factor in the success of communication efforts. You are going to get feedback that you will not like. Don't shy away from responding—a lot of employees are keeping a close eye on how you will react. If leaders do not welcome constructive criticism, employees will not feel obligated or confident to participate. Without the opportunity to provide feedback, employees are more likely to tune out the message. It takes persistence and investment.

Finally, there must be a fair balance between face-to-face communication and online communication. Yes, we live in an overwhelmingly virtual world. But especially in difficult economic times, employees need the reassurance that face-to-face interaction usually brings. Think about it—has a tweet or a blog you've read ever ruined your day? Probably not—but pleasant or unpleasant human interaction can usually make or break it.

**LAURENCE SALMON, RJP ASSET MANAGEMENT SINGAPORE**
Chief executive officer. Speaks Arabic, Japanese, German, and English. Always enjoys a challenge across culture, borders, and languages. Loves to play golf. Favorite saying: Great things come to those who wait.

Where was I to go, and what could I do after the global financial crash in 2008? My position as a CEO with full responsibility to IPO, an asset-based company in Singapore, was in question. What was I to do? Walk away from the company? Stop all activities based on a poor leadership judgment call, or treat this position as a one-off based on market forces, which I could not lead or manage? The banks had little money nor time in their mindset to loan against a company who was in a high-risk game of the oil and gas services industry.

No. I had to find another way, a different way, to raise capital. At that point in my career, I was being approached by Australian executive search companies with offers for other CEO positions. However, one of those companies asked me to use an Internet professional site called LinkedIn where I should put my professional career details for them to access in the future. I was opposed to such advice where anybody in the world on their computers could look at my site and possibly access my leadership integrity.

As a consequence of being logged into this LinkedIn site, however, I surfed its web page and found a company based in the Chicago and New York business world of private equity banking. I approached the CEO/MD of this company via e-mail on what I was doing in Singapore. We interfaced for several weeks where we spoke on Skype as the medium.

After we developed a business plan, financial projections, and bank statements, we were able to create a private equity investment over $120 million. There were no barriers to entry that I knew of or hurdles to challenge on the Internet. It all looked like an easy process to work with across oceans and cultures.

However, prior to the final sign-off of paperwork, I was questioned by the U.S. company as to why my name was referenced on the Internet in a negative manner by an Australian company. I was horrified to read what this company had written about me and the statements made on the web for the world to read.

What had happened was that in 2007 in Australia, I was looking at a management buyout of a company. Based on inconsistencies in their financial records, this deal never took place. Due to my rejecting the deal, this company posted negative comments about me and my integrity, causing a strong questionability of my professionalism.

I lodged a complaint against this company, and I also met in person with several Australian government agencies on this issue of Internet abuse. Australia has no laws on Internet abuse, so the CEO position was put on hold until this matter could be resolved. As a consequence, one of these Australian agencies replied to my complaint stating action will be taken to close that company down.

Verbal abuse was previously relegated to verbal attacks or in print, but the proliferation of technology and the Internet has created the ability for widespread, global slander.

In the sign-off of this Australian government letter, it was stamped by an Australian justice of the peace allowing the U.S. private equity banker to see that my actions are positively in place with my integrity in the United States and are not to be challenged. All correspondence after that clearance was managed via Skype and e-mail transfer again. This problem was respected in the United States, and the relationship was never in question or stopped purely on the basis of the Internet abuse. As a result, in 2010 and 2011, the company I lead as a CEO was listed in the various financial share markets of the United States, the United Arab Emirates, Singapore, and the United Kingdom.

**LU STASKO, STASKO AGENCY**

President. Former companies: WebMaster4Rent, Bing, Zspire, and Prima Research. Was the only American woman who worked for the largest importer of beef to Japan. Was instrumental in getting American Airlines to ship to Japan instead of always using Japanese airlines—a big deal for the export industry. Can ride a unicycle. Hobbies: working out, roller blading, and taking photos of family and friends and then making scrapbooks. Favorite saying: It's all good!

Technology has evolved tremendously since I established my public relations firm, the Stasko Agency, in 1998. When I started my business, I conducted all my calls on a landline, relied on networking events to connect with colleagues and potential new clients, and pitched stories primarily to print and broadcast outlets.

Today, I couldn't survive without my cell phone, and I've expanded my pitch lists to include nontraditional journalism sources, such as bloggers and online-only outlets. Some of my other practices, however, haven't changed. While I use Facebook and other social media platforms to keep up with friends and business associates, I also make a point of networking in person whenever possible because I feel the best form of advertising is for people to see my enthusiasm and energy for what I do.

When it comes to building and maintaining relationships, I still prefer more old-fashioned methods of communication. But I can't deny that technology has helped me disseminate information faster, which is crucial given the fast-paced, 24-hour news cycle.

What works best for me is utilizing a blend of new tools along with more traditional communications vehicles. Tapping into a combination of methods allows me to maintain personal connections, while also equipping me with the ability to deliver information quickly and efficiently when necessary.

For example, I most often use e-mail as a starting point for any correspondence I send to the media, followed by a phone call. I prefer e-mail over simply posting a pitch for a client on

Facebook or Twitter because it's more direct. I also avoid texting because it's difficult to convey a story in such a limited space.

I use e-mail to communicate a wide range of public relations activities. I could be sending a news release, offering a reporter the opportunity to interview a client, or inviting a source to a special event. Because the media are inundated with press releases and story pitches via e-mail, it's essential that whatever message I send be concise and compelling to separate our communications from the others clogging an already full inbox.

The basic facts—the who, what, where, and when—should be listed in the first sentence or two since reporters are short on time. I also avoid sending a lot of attachments with my e-mails since many people now view their e-mail on a smart phone and have trouble downloading documents. It's easier to simply include your message in the body of the e-mail.

Repetition is also key. If I am promoting an event, I utilize a three-prong approach, starting with a save-the-date e-mail, then the actual invitation, and followed by a reminder e-mail the day of the event.

E-mail works well much of the time, but I also make an effort to meet with members of the media to whom I pitch regularly. These chats allow me to gather valuable information about what types of stories are most appealing and the best time to reach out with story ideas. Getting to know reporters on a one-on-one basis also helps me develop a more friendly, informal relationship, which distinguishes me from other practitioners who depend solely on electronic communication. And I'm not above dropping by a television station with goodies to draw attention to a release or client I'm promoting. I've found that it's a fun way to establish name recognition.

When it comes to clients, I believe in personal interaction. I have weekly meetings with nearly all of my clients, conducted by phone, in person or, in one case, via Skype. I also meet personally with any new client before submitting a proposal to provide public relations services. These meetings offer valuable insight into what a company expects to achieve from a public relations campaign, and they help me form a plan to meet those goals.

I am finding that social media can help bridge the gap when personal encounters aren't possible, providing a peek into my busy world. I have a Facebook page for my business, where I provide updates on new clients, client activities, and other business accomplishments. I also have a blog, which offers another avenue to promote my clients as well as my media placements.

I always make sure my clients have a Facebook page because it helps connect them with potential customers and can serve as a place to advertise discounts and special events.

Last, I am a big believer in the lost art of handwritten correspondence. I still send thank-you notes and personally signed holiday cards every year. That effort doesn't go unnoticed. I am always touched when I see one of my cards displayed on a client's desk or receive calls from associates thanking me for thinking of them.

# CONCLUSION

Effective leaders, current and future, have to use every communication tool available to them to get done what needs to be done. Technology and electronic gadgets are just some of those tools. Less tangible but equally essential tools are integrity, attitude, persuasiveness, appearance, and preparation, along with asking questions, making decisions, solving problems, managing others, and connecting to people.

A friend sent me a present that was a full-size computer screen and keyboard made entirely out of edible chocolate. It struck me as the perfect metaphor for what I'm trying to get across in this book: it was a blend of modern machinery with time-proven human self-interest.

The technology we have today—as well as the yet unimagined advancements in the works—is still a tool, not a lifestyle. Learn and utilize every device available to you to the extent it helps, not interferes, with your goals. But never let the gadget get in the way of the human factor. Know how and when to turn on and turn off; gear up and gear down. All it takes is a walk down the hall, so to speak, to correct the wrong an electronic transmission did.

I work all over the world, so I know that universally all people want, and need, to be happy, to love and be loved, to feel smart, and to be valued and appreciated. All of life involves those human interactions. In business, the same human interactions exist, but with money and title attached to them. Today, and going forward, these human interactions take place through advanced technology. Nevertheless, whatever the conduit may be, it is still human-to-human connections. Always has been, always will be.

So when you utilize a device to call, text, e-mail, or video other people, use a thought-through approach to simply and clearly explain: why people should care, what is significant or important, and what's in it for them. Leadership skills like those have nothing to do with a position on an organization chart. With the help of the advanced-technology communication devices in use today, anyone can develop and use these skills and move into leadership positions.

Too many times, people with a lot of technological know-how mistakenly think they don't have to necessarily be gracious and consider others. Wrong. What you do day in and day out in your microcommunications lives with you for an eternity.

Glance back at the end of each chapter and periodically remind yourself about what irritates others so you don't fall into any bad habits. Reread the Online/Offline sections to jog your memory on how to best manage and lead others. Technological advances will fall into your lap on a regular basis, so I don't need to say "keep up" because I know you will.

And constantly remind yourself of the most wonderful thing in life: nobody can ever stop you from getting better.

# SOURCES

The stats highlighted throughout the book came from http://
www: techcrunch.com, press.linkedin.com, marketwire.com,
about-tagged.com, mediapost.com, nytimes.com, blog.hubspot.
com, wsj.com, nielsen.com, usatoday.com, edisonresearch.com,
cnn.com, yahoo.com, and Pew Research.

# INDEX

# ABOUT THE AUTHOR

Debra Benton's focus is to "help you work differently and be different at work; to take you from promise to prominence." Her expertise has given her front-page coverage in the *Wall Street Journal* and *USA Today* (Money), and it has made her a welcome guest on the *Today Show, Good Morning America,* and CNN. She has also been interviewed by Diane Sawyer for CBS.

Condé Nast *Portfolio* magazine described Benton as one of the "top five executive coaches to have on speed dial."

Benton has written for *Harvard Business Review,* the *Wall Street Journal,* and *Bloomberg Businessweek,* and she is the bestselling, award-winning author of eight books.

She is a popular keynote speaker and leadership consultant. A few of her clients include GE, Microsoft, American Express, United Airlines, Time Warner, McKinsey & Company, Verizon, Pfizer, Kraft, Dell, SC Johnson, Lockheed Martin, and the U.S. Border Patrol, as well as individuals from Hollywood to the Washington Beltway.

Benton lives with her husband Rodney Sweeney, a retired cowboy and ranch manager, in Colorado.

Benton is available for executive coaching, training, and keynote presentations. Please visit www.debrabenton.com.